# Microsoft Word 2002
# explained

GW00370510

# Books Available

**By both authors:**
BP341 MS-DOS explained
BP346 Programming in Visual Basic for Windows
BP388 Why not personalise your PC
BP400 Windows 95 explained
BP406 MS Word 95 explained
BP407 Excel 95 explained
BP408 Access 95 one step at a time
BP409 MS Office 95 one step at a time
BP420 E-mail on the Internet*
BP426 MS-Office 97 explained
BP428 MS-Word 97 explained
BP429 MS-Excel 97 explained
BP430 MS-Access 97 one step at a time
BP433 Your own Web site on the Internet
BP448 Lotus SmartSuite 97 explained
BP456 Windows 98 explained*
BP460 Using Microsoft Explorer 4 on the Internet*
BP464 E-mail and news with Outlook Express*
BP465 Lotus SmartSuite Millennium explained
BP471 Microsoft Office 2000 explained
BP472 Microsoft Word 2000 explained
BP473 Microsoft Excel 2000 explained
BP474 Microsoft Access 2000 explained
BP478 Microsoft Works 2000 explained
BP486 Using Linux the easy way*
BP488 Internet Explorer 5 explained*
BP487 Quicken 2000 UK explained*
BP491 Windows 2000 explained*
BP493 Windows Me explained*
BP498 Using Visual Basic
BP505 Microsoft Works Suite 2001 explained
BP509 Microsoft Office XP explained
BP510 Microsoft Word 2002 explained
BP511 Microsoft Excel 2002 explained
BP512 Microsoft Access 2002 explained

**By Noel Kantaris:**
BP258 Learning to Program in C
BP259 A Concise Introduction to UNIX*
BP284 Programming in QuickBASIC
BP325 A Concise User's Guide to Windows 3.1

# Microsoft Word 2002 explained

## by

## P.R.M. Oliver
## and
## N. Kantaris

Bernard Babani (publishing) Ltd
The Grampians
Shepherds Bush Road
London W6 7NF
England

*www.babanibooks.com*

# Please Note

Although every care has been taken with the production of this book to ensure that any projects, designs, modifications and/or programs, etc., contained herewith, operate in a correct and safe manner and also that any components specified are normally available in Great Britain, the Publishers and Author(s) do not accept responsibility in any way for the failure (including fault in design) of any project, design, modification or program to work correctly or to cause damage to any equipment that it may be connected to or used in conjunction with, or in respect of any other damage or injury that may be so caused, nor do the Publishers accept responsibility in any way for the failure to obtain specified components.

Notice is also given that if equipment that is still under warranty is modified in any way or used or connected with home-built equipment then that warranty may be void.

British Library Cataloguing in Publication Data:

A catalogue record for this book is available from the British Library

ISBN 0 85934 510 6

Cover Design by Gregor Arthur
Printed and Bound in Great Britain by Cox & Wyman Ltd, Reading

# About this Book

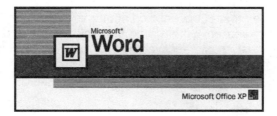

*Microsoft Word 2002 explained* has been written to help users to get to grips with Microsoft's latest word processor, which is also a desk top publishing and Internet publishing package, in the fastest possible time.

No previous knowledge is assumed, but the book does not describe how to install and use Microsoft Windows itself. If you need to know more about Windows, then may we suggest you select a book from the 'Books Available' list. They are all published by BERNARD BABANI (publishing) Ltd.

*Microsoft Word 2002* is part of the Office XP package and is an exciting new application that will help you make really professional documents and presentations, both personal and for business. It offers new tools that use Web technology to provide enhanced workgroup productivity and the ability to access and publish information on the Internet (including the 'almost effortless' design of your Web site). Building on Word 2000, Microsoft has made Word 2002 documents more browser-readable when you save them as Web pages. Such Web pages are then fully functional Word documents which makes publishing them a live activity.

This book introduces Word 2002 with sufficient detail to get you working, then discusses how to share information between programs, and how to use the built-in Internet features. No prior knowledge of the package's capabilities is assumed.

The book was written with the busy person in mind. It is not necessary to learn all there is to know about a subject, when reading a few selected pages can usually do the same thing quite adequately. With the help of this book, it is hoped that you will be able to come to terms with Microsoft Word 2002 and get the most out of your computer in terms of efficiency, productivity and enjoyment, and that you will be able to do it in the shortest, most effective and informative way.

If you would like to purchase a Companion Disc for any of the listed books by the same author(s), apart from the ones marked with an asterisk, containing the file/program listings which appear in them, then fill in the form at the back of the book and send it to Phil Oliver at the stipulated address.

# About the Authors

**Phil Oliver** graduated in Mining Engineering at Camborne School of Mines in 1967 and since then has specialised in most aspects of surface mining technology, with a particular emphasis on computer related techniques. He has worked in Guyana, Canada, several Middle Eastern countries, South Africa and the United Kingdom, on such diverse projects as: the planning and management of bauxite, iron, gold and coal mines; rock excavation contracting in the UK; international mining equipment sales and international mine consulting for a major mining house in South Africa. In 1988 he took up a lecturing position at Camborne School of Mines (part of Exeter University) in Surface Mining and Management. He retired from full-time lecturing in 1998, to spend more time writing, consulting and developing Web sites for clients.

**Noel Kantaris** graduated in Electrical Engineering at Bristol University and after spending three years in the Electronics Industry in London, took up a Tutorship in Physics at the University of Queensland. Research interests in Ionospheric Physics, led to the degrees of M.E. in Electronics and Ph.D. in Physics. On return to the UK, he took up a Post-Doctoral Research Fellowship in Radio Physics at the University of Leicester, and then in 1973 a lecturing position in Engineering at the Camborne School of Mines, Cornwall, (part of Exeter University), where between 1978 and 1997 he was also the CSM Computing Manager. At present he is IT Director of FFC Ltd.

# Acknowledgements

We would like to thank the staff of Microsoft Press Centre for providing the software programs on which this work was based.

# Trademarks

**Arial** and **Times New Roman** are registered trademarks of The Monotype Corporation plc.

**EPSON** is a registered trademark of Seiko Epson Corporation.

**HP and LaserJet** are registered trademarks of Hewlett Packard Corporation.

**IBM** is a registered trademark of International Business Machines, Inc.

**Intel** is a registered trademark of Intel Corporation.

**Microsoft**, **MS-DOS**, **Office XP**, **Windows**, **Windows NT**, **Windows Me** and **Visual Basic**, are either registered trademarks or trademarks of Microsoft Corporation.

**PostScript** is a registered trademark of Adobe Systems Incorporated.

**TrueType** is a registered trademark of Apple Corporation.

All other brand and product names used in the book are recognised as trademarks, or registered trademarks, of their respective companies.

# Contents

# 1

# Package Overview

Microsoft's Word 2002 is part of the Office XP package and is without doubt the best Windows word processor so far. As you would expect, it is fully integrated with all the other Office XP applications. This version of Word, like its predecessors, has particularly strong leanings towards desk top publishing which offers fully editable WYSIWYG (what you see is what you get) modes that can be viewed in various zoom levels. Couple this with the ability to include and manipulate full colour graphics and to easily create Web pages and you can see the enormous power of the program. You will find using Word 2002 to be even more intuitive and easy than earlier versions and you will soon be producing the type of word processed output you would not have dreamt possible.

In many situations Word 2002 will attempt to anticipate what you want to do and will probably produce the correct result most of the time. For example, AutoCorrect and AutoFormat can, when active, correct common spelling mistakes and format documents automatically. Other Wizards can help you with everyday tasks and/or make complex tasks easier to manage.

Word uses Object Linking and Embedding (OLE) to move and share information seamlessly between Office XP applications. For example, you can drag information from one application to another, or you can link information from one application into another. Similarly, Hyperlinks can be used from any of the Office XP applications to access other Office documents, files on an internal or external Web or FTP (File Transfer Protocol) site, or HTML (Hypertext Markup Language) files. Hyperlinks help you use your documents with the Internet.

Finally, writing macros in Visual Basic gives you a powerful development platform with which to create custom solutions.

# Hardware and Software Requirements

If Microsoft Word 2002 is already installed on your computer, you can safely skip this and the following section of this chapter.

To install and use Word 2002, which comes as part of Microsoft Office XP, you need an IBM-compatible PC. Microsoft suggests at least a 133 MHz Pentium processor for the installation of the Standard edition of Office XP which includes Outlook, Word, Excel, and PowerPoint. In addition, you need the following:

- Windows 98, Me, XT, NT4, or 2000 Professional as the operating system. If you have Windows 95 or older you will need to upgrade your system!

- Random access memory (RAM) required is:

  *For Windows 98*, 24 MB plus 8 MB for each Office application running at the same time.

  *For Windows Me or NT*, 32 MB plus 8 MB for each Office application running at the same time.

  *For Windows 2000*, 64 MB plus 8 MB for each Office application running at the same time.

- Hard disc space required for the Standard edition of Office XP is 245 MB, but this varies with your system.

- CD-ROM drive.

- SuperVGA (800 x 600) or higher screen resolution with at least 256-colour display.

- Pointing device: Microsoft Mouse or compatible.

Realistically, to run the above mentioned Office XP applications, including Word 2002, with reasonable sized documents, you will need the most powerful Pentium PC with at least 128 MB of RAM. To run Microsoft Office XP from a network, you must also have a network compatible with your

Windows operating environment, such as Microsoft's Windows 98 or higher, Windows NT4, LAN Manager, etc.

Finally, if you are connected to the Internet, you can take advantage of the extra help located on Microsoft's Web sites, or use Word's advanced editing and formatting features when working with e-mail messages. To use Word 2002 as your e-mail editor, you must have Microsoft Outlook 2002 installed on your computer.

# Installing Microsoft Office XP

Installing Office XP on your computer is done with the Setup program, located on the program CD-ROM.

**Note:** If you are using a virus detection utility, disable it before running Setup, as it might conflict with it.

To install Microsoft Office XP, place the distribution CD in your CD drive and close it. The auto-start program on the CD will start the Setup program automatically. If that does not work, click the **Start** button, and select the **Run** command which opens the Run dialogue box, shown in Fig. 1.1 below.

Next, type in the **Open** box:

```
G:\setup
```

as shown here.

In this case we used the CD-ROM in the G: drive; yours could well be a different drive. Clicking the **OK** button, starts the

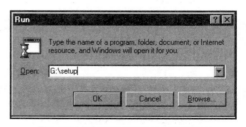

Fig. 1.1 Using the Windows Run Box

installation of Microsoft Office XP. Setup displays the first of several screens.

We suggest that you follow the instructions displayed on the screen. With us Setup went through the following procedure:

You are prompted to type your name and the name of your organisation (optional) and then the 25-character Product Key for your version of the program. If you haven't found this it is on the back of the CD case. Then move to the second box by pressing the **Next** button.

You are then asked to accept the licence agreement and passed to the box shown here in Fig. 1.2.

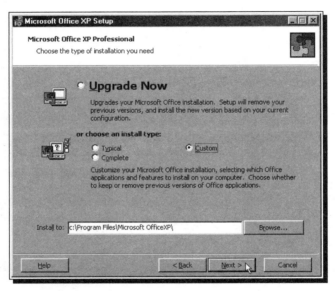

Fig. 1.2 Selecting the Type of Installation

If you are happy to do it, the easiest way is to select the default **Upgrade Now** option. But if, like us, you want to make sure everything works before losing your previous version of Office, we suggest you select the **Custom** option and enter a new folder destination to hold the new package. Obviously to do this you will need extra hard disc space, but with modern machines that should not be too much of a problem.

In the next box select the Office applications you want to install and click the **Choose detailed installation options for each application** option, before clicking on **Next**.

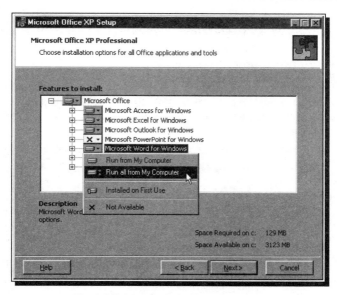

Fig. 1.3 Selecting the Features to Install

The next box, shown in Fig. 1.3, lets you select exactly the features you want for each application. Clicking the **Help** button will explain all the features here, as shown in our Fig. 1.4 below.

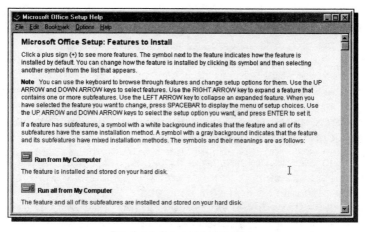

Fig. 1.4 A Setup Help Window

To avoid having to access the Office CD every time you want to use one of the extra Word features we suggest you make sure that all the options under Microsoft Word are set to **Run from My Computer**.

The next box (not shown here) lets you choose which older Office programs you want to keep on your PC (if any). You do not get the choice with Outlook, as the new Outlook 2002 is 'mandatory'.

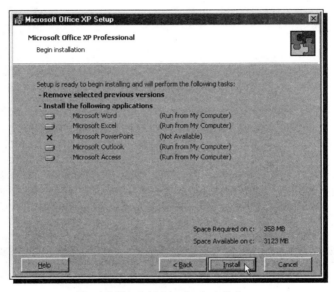

Fig. 1.5 Check List for the Installation

The next dialogue box (Fig. 1.5) lists what will be removed and installed. If you are not happy with anything here, press the **Back** button and make any required changes. Otherwise press **Install** to start the operation.

With both of our first time installations we were asked to insert the CD of the previous version of Office, and were later presented with an error message about a missing file. All this meant was that Setup was expecting the Office XP CD to be in the drive again, but had not asked for it to be replaced. Easy to rectify once you know how.

Fig. 1.6 Finished at Last!

Hopefully you will eventually be presented with the message box shown in Fig. 1.6. We found it worth the effort though.

The Setup program modifies your system files automatically so that you can start Word easily by creating and displaying a new entry in the **Start, Programs** cascade menu.

In addition, Office XP adds two entries to the top section of the Windows **Start** menu; the **New Office Document**, and the **Open Office Document**. The first allows you to select in a displayed dialogue box the tab containing the type of document you want to work with, such as letters & faxes, memos, or presentations, to mention but a few. Double-clicking the type of document or template you want, automatically loads the appropriate application. The second entry allows you to work with existing documents. Opening a document, first starts the application originally used to create it, then opens the document in it.

# Activating Your Software

In an effort to restrict the 'illegal' use of their software, Microsoft have introduced an activation procedure with Office XP. You can only use it more than fifty times if you complete this activation procedure by phone, or over the Internet. It also means that you can only use XP on one machine. Perhaps times are getting harder at Microsoft.

When you first open Word 2002 you may be presented with the box shown in Fig. 1.7.

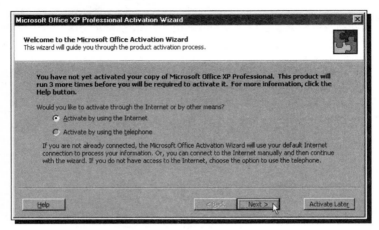

Fig. 1.7 The Activation Wizard

If so, you will have to follow the Wizard's instructions. We found the easiest way was to log on to the Internet and then work through the five dialogue boxes that were presented. The only information that was essential was the country we were using the software in.

Apparently the activation procedure marries up the product key details of the software with the hardware setup of your computer. This makes a unique combination, and Microsoft will not let that software be activated on another computer at the same time. In fact, if you re-format your hard disc, or change your hardware installation too much, you will have to re-activate the software. The only consolation is that the procedure is fairly quick and painless.

# Adding or Removing Office Applications

To add or remove an Office application, left-click the Windows **Start** button at the bottom left corner of the screen, point to **Settings**, then click the **Control Panel** option on the Windows pop-up menu.

This opens the Control Panel dialogue box. Next, double-click the Add/Remove Programs icon, shown here to the left, to open the dialogue box shown in Fig. 1.8 below. Click the Install/Uninstall tab and select the Microsoft Office XP program, and then click the **Add/Remove** button.

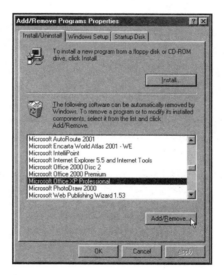

Fig. 1.8 The Add/Remove Programs Box

Office Setup will then display the Maintenance Mode dialogue box shown overleaf in Fig. 1.9. You will need to insert the Office XP CD into your CD drive to carry out most of the functions offered.

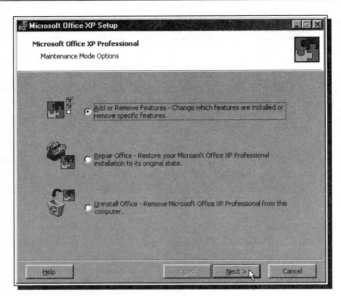

Fig. 1.9 Office XP Maintenance Mode Dialogue Box

Selecting **Add or Remove Features** opens up the dialogue box shown in Fig. 1.3 in which you can select which Office applications and features you want installed.

Note the additional buttons on the above screen. Use the **Repair Office** button to reinstall the whole of Office XP, or to find and fix any errors in your original installation.

Finally, you can use the **Uninstall Office** button to uninstall all of the Office XP applications.

# New Word 2002 Features

**Task panes** - Some of the most common tasks in Word are now organised in panes that display alongside your working document. You can, for instance, quickly create new documents or open files using the task pane that appears when you start Word, or continue working while you search for a file using the Search task pane, or pick from a gallery of items to paste in the Office Clipboard task pane.

**Ask a Question box** - When you want help you can type a question in this new box, located on the menu bar, and get a list of Help choices.

**Smart tags** - New in-place buttons let you immediately adjust how information is pasted or how automatic changes are made by Word.

**Updated Clip Organiser** - (Formerly the Clip Gallery). Has hundreds of new clip art files and an easy task pane interface.

**Improved handling of pictures and drawings** - Word uses a new graphics system which gives shapes and WordArt much smoother outlines, as well as adjustable levels of transparency and true blending. Digital images now stay sharper and clearer when they are resized.

**Digital signatures** - You can apply a digital signature to a file to confirm that it has not been altered.

**Save a Web page as a single file** - A special Web archive file format is available which lets you save all the elements of a Web page, including text and graphics, into a single file.

**Document recovery and safer shutdown** - Current documents can be recovered if Word encounters an error or stops responding. They are displayed in the Document Recovery task pane the next time you open the program.

**Office Safe Mode** - Office XP programs can now detect and isolate start-up problems. This lets you get round the problem, run Word in safe mode, and continue working.

**Crash reporting tool** - Diagnostic information about program crashes can be collected and sent to your IT department or to Microsoft itself, allowing problems to be corrected in the easiest way.

**Formatting improvements** - The Styles and Formatting task pane can be used to create, view, select, apply, or clear formatting from text. Whilst the Reveal Formatting task pane lets you display text formatting attributes, Word also marks formatting inconsistencies with blue, wavy underlines.

**AutoCorrect and Paste Options buttons** appear directly in your document to help you fine-tune these tasks. This means you can control automatic correction and pasting operations without having to click a toolbar button or use a dialogue box.

**Collaborative document creation** - An improved Reviewing toolbar can be used for document collaboration.

**Speech recognition** - It is now possible (but not in the UK) to use speech recognition to select menu, toolbar, dialogue box, and task pane items by using your voice.

**Handwriting recognition** - You can write with a handwriting input device (such as a graphics tablet) and use handwriting recognition to enter the text into a document. The natural handwriting can be converted to typed characters or left as hand-written text, such as a signature.

**Improved table and list formatting** - Word now offers drag-and-drop copying of tables, custom table and list styles, and improved sorting. You can also format bullets or numbers independently of the text in a list.

**Enhanced AutoComplete** - The name of any person you send e-mail to in Outlook 2002 will later be recognised in Word and used as an AutoComplete suggestion.

**Multi-selection** - You can now select non-contiguous areas of a document, which makes it easy to format text in different places.

**Improved word count** - With the Word Count toolbar, you can continuously check the word count in a document without having to repeatedly open a dialogue box.

**Simplified mail merge** - Word now uses a task pane to provide a new way to connect to your data source and create form letters, mailing labels, envelopes, directories, and mass e-mail and fax distributions.

**Hiding white space** - In print layout view you can now reduce wasted space on the screen by hiding the white space at the top and bottom of a document.

**Drawing Canvas** - The new Drawing Canvas helps you easily insert, position, layer, and re-size drawing objects.

**Diagramming** - You can add a variety of diagrams using the diagramming tools on the Drawing toolbar.

**Improved watermarks** - It is now easy to select a picture, logo, or text to use as the background to a printed document.

**Improved cascading style sheets** - You can use Word to attach, remove, and manage cascading style sheets. This provides a convenient way to format several Web pages or a whole Web site.

**Improved picture bullets** - Picture bullets now behave just like other bullets in Word and can be used for different levels.

**Filtered HTML** - To reduce the size of Web pages and e-mail messages in HTML format, you can now save them in filtered HTML so that the tags used by Microsoft Office programs are removed.

**Translation** - Word offers a basic bilingual dictionary and translation capability in both French and Spanish.

**Symbols and international characters** - Word now offers improved ways to add these types of characters to your document, either through the improved Symbol dialogue box, or by using <ALT+X> keyboard shortcuts.

Most of these new features of Word 2002 will be examined in the following chapters of this book. Whenever possible, we introduce practical examples that you are encouraged to type in and use to illustrate particular points, and then save on disc for future use.

# 2

# The Word Environment

There are several ways to start the Word program. You can click the Windows **Start** button, select **Programs** and then click on the 'Microsoft Word' entry in the cascade menu, as shown in Fig. 2.1 below.

Fig. 2.1 The Windows Start Menu System

When it is installed, Office XP adds two entries to the top section of the Windows **Start** menu; **New Office Document**, and **Open Office Document** as shown above. These can be used to create new Word documents and to open existing ones as explained on page 7. Also just double-clicking on a Word document file in a 'My Computer' window will open Word with the document loaded.

Our favourite method is to create a shortcut on the Windows desktop, as shown in Fig. 2.1. This is easily done by highlighting the Word entry in the cascade menu, as shown above, dragging the pointer to the desktop with the right mouse button depressed, and selecting the **Create Shortcut(s) Here** option when the button is released.

# The Word Screen

The opening 'blank' screen of Word 2002 is shown below. It is perhaps worth spending some time looking at the various parts that make up this screen. Word follows the usual Microsoft Windows conventions and if you are familiar with these you can skip some of this section, but even so, a few minutes might be well spent here.

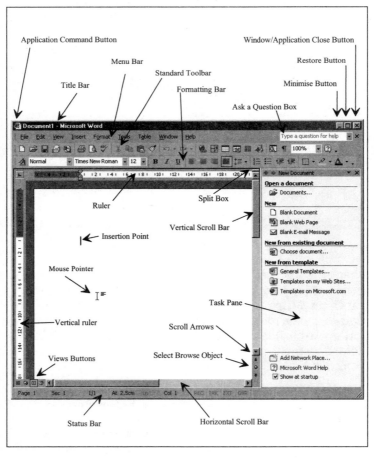

Fig. 2.2 The Word Screen Layout

The layout as shown is in a window, but if you click on the application restore button, you can make Word take up the full screen area available. Using a window can be useful when you are running several applications at the same time and you want to transfer between them with the mouse.

Note that in this case, the Word window displays an empty document with the title 'Document1', and has a solid 'Title bar', indicating that it is the active application window. Although multiple windows can be displayed simultaneously, you can only enter data into the active window (which will always be displayed on top unless you view them with a split screen). Title bars of non active windows appear a lighter shade than that of the active one.

The Word screen is divided into several areas which have the following functions:

| *Area* | *Function* |
|---|---|
| Command buttons | Clicking on the command button, (see upper-left corner of the Word window), displays a pull-down menu which can be used to control the program window. It allows you to restore, move, size, minimise, maximise, and close the window. |
| Title Bar | The bar at the top of a window which displays the application name and the name of the current document. |
| Minimise Button | When clicked on, this button minimises Word to an icon on the Windows Taskbar. |
| Restore Button | When clicked on, this button restores the active window to the position and size that was occupied before it |

was maximised. The restore button is then replaced by a Maximise button, as shown here, which is used to set the window to full screen size.

Close button

The extreme top right button that you click to close a window.

Menu Bar

The bar below the Title bar which allows you to choose from several menu options. Clicking on a menu item displays the pull-down menu associated with that item.

Ask a Question Box

The text box at the far right of the menu bar. You can type in a help query and press the Return key to get a listing of matching topics.

Standard Toolbar

The bar below the Menu bar which contains buttons that give you mouse click access to the functions most often used in the program.

Formatting Bar

The buttons on the Formatting Bar allow you to change the attributes of a font, such as italic and underline, and also to format text in various ways. The Formatting Bar contains three boxes; a style box, a font box and a size box to give instant access to all the installed styles, fonts and character sizes.

Rulers

The horizontal and vertical bars where you can see and set page margins, tabulation points and indents.

| | |
|---|---|
| Split Box | The area above the top vertical scroll button which when dragged allows you to split the screen. |
| Task Pane | A new pane which presents formatting options and other relevant controls on the right-hand side of the Word screen. It has its own button bar for instant control. |
| Scroll Bars | The areas on the screen that contain scroll boxes in vertical and horizontal bars. Clicking on these bars allows you to control the part of a document which is visible on the screen. |
| Scroll Arrows | The arrowheads at each end of each scroll bar which you can click to scroll the screen up and down one line, or left and right 10% of the screen, at a time. |
| Insertion pointer | The pointer used to indicate where text will be inserted. |
| Views Buttons | Clicking these buttons changes screen views quickly. |
| Status Bar | The bottom line of the document window that displays status information. |

# The Toolbars

There are nineteen different toolbars available in Word 2002. To see the full list you can use the **View**, **Toolbars** menu command, or more easily, right-click in the toolbar area. In this list active bars are shown with a blue tick to their left. Clicking on a list entry will toggle that toolbar on or off. By default, only two bars are active, the Standard and the Formatting toolbars.

When Word is first opened these two bars will probably be placed alongside each other, which means that not all the buttons (or icons) will be visible. To see the other available buttons click the toolbar options button at the right end of each bar, as shown in Fig. 2.3.

Fig. 2.3 Toolbar Options

Clicking any of the buttons now displayed will action that function. For our screen layout of Fig. 2.2 we have clicked the **Show Buttons on Two Rows** option, as shown above. We find it easier to work with both toolbars almost fully open. The best thing is to play around here and find the settings that suit you best.

To 'complicate' matters further, Word 2002 automatically customises both toolbars and menus, based on how often you use their commands. As you work, they adjust so that only the buttons and commands you use most often are shown. Thus you may not see exactly the same features displayed on your screen, as shown here.

## The Standard Toolbar

As we show it, this is located below the Menu bar at the top of the Word screen and contains command buttons. As you move the mouse pointer over a button it changes to an 'active' blue colour and a banner opens to indicate the button's function. Left-clicking the button will then action that function or command.

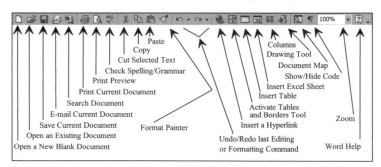

Fig. 2.4 Standard Toolbar Functions

## The Formatting Bar

This is located to the right of, or below, the Standard Toolbar, and is divided into sections that contain command buttons, as shown in Fig. 2.5 below.

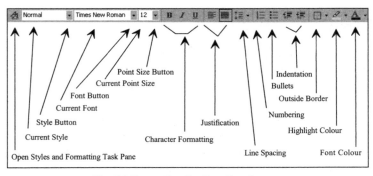

Fig. 2.5 Formatting Toolbar Functions

The first option displays the name of the current style (Normal) in a box. Clicking the down-arrow against this box, opens up a menu of default paragraph styles with their font sizes. The Current font box shows the current typeface. Clicking on the down-arrow button to the right of it allows you to change the typeface of any selected text. The Current point size box shows the size of selected characters which can be changed by clicking on the down-arrow button next to it and selecting another size from the displayed list.

Next, are three character formatting buttons which allow you to enhance selected text by emboldening, italicising, or underlining it. The next buttons allow you to change the justification of a selected paragraph, control the Line spacing and set the different types of Numbering and Indentation options. The last three buttons allow you to add an Outside Border to selected text or objects, and change the highlight and font colour of selected text.

## The Status Bar

This is located at the bottom of the Word window and is used to display statistics about the active document.

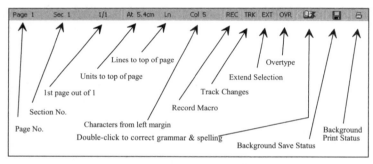

Fig. 2.6 The Word Status Bar

For example, when a document is being opened, the Status bar displays for a short time its name and length in terms of total number of characters. Once a document is opened, the Status bar displays the statistics of the document at the insertion point; here it is on Page 1, Section 1, and 5 characters from the left margin.

Double-clicking the left of the status bar displays the Find and Replace dialogue box, as shown in Fig. 2.7 on the next page. This is shown with the **Go To** tab selected. You can choose which page, section line, etc., of the document to go to, or you can use the other tabs to **Find** and **Replace** text (more about this later).

Double-clicking the other features on the Status bar will also activate their features.

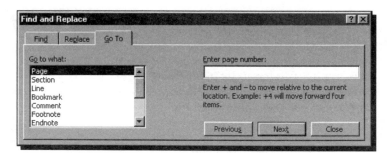

Fig. 2.7 The Find and Replace Box

## The Menu Bar Options

Each menu bar option has associated with it a pull-down sub-menu. To activate the menu, either press the <Alt> key, which causes the first option of the menu (in this case the **File** menu option) to be selected, then use the right and left arrow keys to highlight any of the options in the menu, or use the mouse to point to an option. Pressing either the <Enter> key, or the left mouse button, reveals the pull-down sub-menu of the highlighted menu option. The sub-menu of the **File** option is shown below.

Fig. 2.8 The File Sub Menu

Note that as in the previous version of Word, the drop-down sub-menu displays only the most important options, but you have the option to view the full sub-menu by highlighting the double arrow-heads at the bottom of it, by either pointing to that part of the sub-menu with the mouse or using the down-arrow cursor key to move the highlighted bar down.

The full sub-menu of the **File** menu option is displayed here. However, the order of your sub-menu options in both the short and the full version of the sub-menu could differ from ours. This is because Word learns from your actions and auto-matically promotes the items you choose from menu extensions on to the shortened version of the sub-menu.

Fig. 2.9
The Full File Sub Menu

Menu options can also be activated directly by pressing the <Alt> key followed by the underlined letter of the required option. Thus, pressing <Alt+F>, opens the pull-down **File** sub-menu. You can use the up and down arrow keys to move the highlighted bar up and down a sub-menu, or the right and left arrow keys to move along the options in the menu bar. Pressing the <Enter> key selects the highlighted option or executes the highlighted command. Pressing the <Esc> key once, closes the pull-down sub-menu, while pressing the <Esc> key for a second time, closes the menu system.

Some of the sub-menu options can be accessed with 'quick key' combinations from the keyboard. Such combinations are shown on the drop-down menus, for example, <Ctrl+S> is the quick key for the **Save** option in the **File** sub-menu. If a sub-menu option is not available, at any time, it will display in a grey colour. Some menu options only appear in Word when that tool is being used, but the ones described below remain constant.

The following is a brief description of the standard menu options. For a more detailed description of each sub-menu item, use the on-line **Help** system (to be described shortly).

**File**    Produces a pull-down menu of mainly file related tasks, such as creating a **New** document, the ability to **Open**, or **Close** files, and **Save** files with the same name, or **Save As** a different name, or even **Save as Web Page**. You can use **Search** to open the Search For Task pane, **Web Page Preview** to open the current page in Explorer, **Page Setup** to set the margins and the size of your printed page, **Print Preview** a document on screen before committing it to paper, or **Print** a document and select your current printer. You can direct documents to other users who share resources with you, using the **Send To** option, view a specific file's **Properties**, and finally, you can **Exit** the program.

**Edit**    Produces a pull-down menu which allows you to **Undo** changes made, **Cut**, **Copy** and **Paste** text and graphics, open the **Office Clipboard** Task pane, **Paste Special** formatting effects, or as a **Hyperlink**. To **Clear** formatting or selections and to **Select All** the contents of a document, or **Find** specific text in a document and **Replace** text, to **Go to** to any location in a document, to view and update **Links**, or open a selected **Object**.

**View**    Produces a pull-down menu which contains screen display options which allow you to change the editing view to **Normal**, **Web Layout**, **Print Layout** or **Outline**. Lets you open the **Task Pane**, control whether to display the **Toolbars**, or the **Ruler**, and to show the working file as a **Document Map**.

Has options to show a list of **Headers/ Footers**, to open windows for viewing **Footnotes** or **Markup** comments, to display in **Full Screen** mode and to set the scale of the editing view with the **Zoom** option.

**Insert**

Produces a pull-down menu which allows you to insert **Breaks** to the ends of pages, columns, or sections, add **Page Numbers** to a document, or insert the **Date and Time**. You can also insert or define **AutoText** items of frequently used text or graphics, insert a **Field** (instruction) for computed contents, or insert special characters with **Symbol**. Further, you can insert a note and activate the **Comment** pane, or insert various types of **References** or **Web Components** into your document. Finally, you can insert a **Picture**, a **Diagram**, a **Text Box**, the contents of a **File**, or an **Object** into the active document and assign a name (**Bookmark**) to a section of your document, or insert **Hyperlinks** to other documents.

**Format**

Produces a pull-down menu which allows you to alter the appearance of text, both on the screen and when printed. Such features as **Font**, size, colour, alignment, print spacing, justification, and enhancements (bold, underlined and italic) are included. You can change the indent and spacing of a selected **Paragraph**, create bullet or number lists and change the numbering options for heading level styles, change the **Borders and Shading** of a selected paragraph, table cell(s), or picture, or change the **Columns** format of the selected section.

You can also set and clear **Tabs**, format the first character of a paragraph as a **Drop Cap**(ital), change **Text Direction**, and

**Change Case**. You can further set the **Background** colour, add a **Theme**, a **Frame**, select options to **AutoFormat** a document, browse and apply or modify **Stylesand Formatting**, or change the fill, line, size and position of a selected **Object**.

Tools Produces a pull-down menu that gives access to the **Spelling and Grammar** checker, lets you change the **Language** formatting of the selected characters. You can also display the **Word Count** statistics of the current document, **Autosummarize** selected text, open **Look Up Reference** documents (if you have them), and in some countries (but not the UK) activate the **Speech** recognition feature.

You can further **Track Changes** to a document, **Compare and Merge** and **Protect** documents, activate **Online Collaboration**, use the **Letters and Mailings** option to create and print letters, envelopes and labels and the new Mail Merge feature. Finally, you can access Microsoft's **Tools on the Web** pages, run, create, delete or edit a **Macro** (a set of instructions), control your document's styles **Templates and Add-Ins**, the **AutoCorrect Options**, you can **Customize** Word to your own requirements and change various Word **Options**.

Table You can use the **Draw Table** or **Insert**, **Table** options of this pull-down menu to create a table of specified rows and columns at the insertion point. Once a table exists, many other options become available to you. From here you can **Insert**, **Delete**, and **Select** the table, or its rows, columns or cells, **Merge Cells** and **Split Cells**, or the table itself.

Further, you can select the **Table AutoFormat** option to choose from a set of pre-formatted table styles and have them applied to your table, use **AutoFit** to change the heights and widths of rows and columns automatically, and toggle the table **Headings** attribute on and off. Finally, you can select a section of text and use the **Convert** option to have it incorporated into a table, or vice versa, rearrange a selection into a specified **Sort** order, insert a **Formula** in a cell, toggle the table **Gridlines** on and off, and open the **Table Properties** dialogue box.

**W**indow     Produces a menu to open a **New Window**, and control the display of existing open windows on the screen.

**H**elp     Activates the help menu which you can use to access the **Microsoft Word Help**, **Hide/ Show the Office Assistant**, the **What's This** facility, or the **Office on the Web** option (if you are connected to the Internet). The **Activate Product** option is needed to use Word once it is installed, you can get **WordPerfect Help** if you are converting from that program, **Detect and Repair** errors in Word, or use the **About Microsoft Word** option to open up a dialogue box from which you can find out information about your version of Word, your system, or get information on Technical Support.

To get more details about any of the above menu options, simply highlight the option and use the <Shift+F1> key combination. This opens a pop-up box like that shown here for the **T**ools, **Options** menu.

> **Options (Tools menu)**
> Modifies settings for Microsoft Office programs such as screen appearance, printing, editing, spelling, and other options.

# Task Panes

Some of the common tasks in Word 2002 can now be carried out in new task panes that display on the right side of your document. You can quickly create new documents or open files using the task pane that appears when you first start the program. The Search task pane gives you easy access to Word's file search facilities, or you can visually pick from a gallery of items in the Office Clipboard task pane.

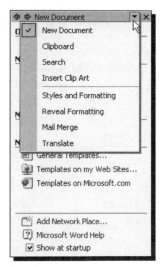

Fig. 2.10 shows the New Document task pane with its control buttons on top. The left and right arrows let you quickly move between the task panes you have open, the down arrow opens a drop-down list of the available tasks, as shown here. The x button lets you close the pane. To re-open it you use the **View**, **Task Pane** menu command.

Fig. 2.10
The Task Pane List

We must admit to having reservations about this new feature of Office XP, but once you get used to the panes, they 'become less of a pain' and at times can make some of Word's features much easier and quicker to access. Each type of pane will be discussed in more detail as they are encountered throughout the book.

# Shortcut Menus

Context-sensitive shortcut menus are now one of Windows' most useful features. If you click the right mouse button on any screen feature, or document, a shortcut menu is displayed with the most frequently used commands relating to the type of work you were doing at the time. In this version of Word, Microsoft have also combined 'smart tags' as part of the shortcut menu system. These automatically link related features or data to the situation involved.

The composite screen dump in Fig. 2.11 below shows in turn the shortcut menus that open when selected text, or the Toolbar area is right-clicked. In the first shortcut menu the **Cut** and **Copy** commands only become effective if you have text selected.

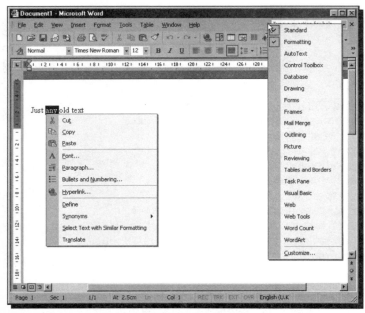

Fig. 2.11 Example Shortcut Menus

So, whatever you are doing in Word, you have rapid access to a menu of relevant functions by right-clicking your mouse. Left-clicking the mouse on an open menu selection will choose that function, while clicking on an area outside the shortcut menu (or pressing the <Esc> key), closes down the shortcut menu. If you are wondering about the smart tags we mentioned, don't worry we will get round to them a little later on.

## Dialogue Boxes

Three periods after a sub-menu option or command, means that a dialogue box will open when the option or command is selected. A dialogue box is used for the insertion of additional information, such as the name of a file or path.

 To see a dialogue box, click the **Open** toolbar button shown here, press <Alt+F>, and select the **Open** option, or use the <Ctrl+O> shortcut keystrokes. With all of these, the Open dialogue box is displayed, as shown in Fig. 2.12 below.

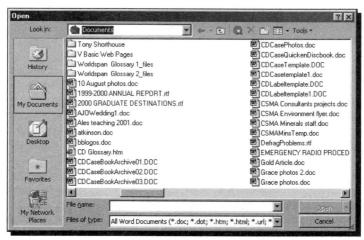

Fig. 2.12 The Open Dialogue Box

When a dialogue box opens, the easiest way to move around it is by clicking with the mouse, otherwise the <Tab> key can be used to move the cursor from one column in the box to another (<Shift+Tab> moves the cursor backwards). Alternatively you can move directly to a desired field by holding the <Alt> key down and pressing the underlined letter in the field name.

Within a column of options you can click with the mouse, or use the arrow keys to move from one to another. Having selected an option or typed in information, you must press a command button such as the **Open** or **Cancel** button, or choose from additional options. In our example note that the **Open** option is not available, as we have not yet selected a file from the list.

Once this is corrected, to select the **Open** button with the mouse, simply click on it, while with the keyboard you must first press the <Tab> key until the dotted rectangle, or focus, moves to the required button, and then press the <Enter> key. Pressing <Enter> at any time while a dialogue box is open, will cause the marked items to be selected and the box to be closed.

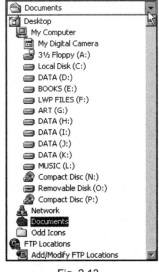

Some dialogue boxes contain List boxes which show a column of available choices, similar to the one at the top of the previous screen dump which appears by pressing the down-arrow button, as shown here in Fig. 2.13.

Fig. 2.13
A List Box

If there are more choices than can be seen in the area provided, use the scroll bars to reveal them. To select a single item from a List box, either double-click the item, or use the arrow keys to highlight the item and press <Enter>.

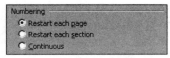

Fig. 2.14 Option Buttons

Other dialogue boxes contain Option buttons with a list of mutually exclusive items, as shown in Fig. 2.14.

The default choice is marked with a black dot against its name, while unavailable options are dimmed.

Other dialogue boxes contain Check boxes, like the one in Fig. 2.15, which offer a list of options you can switch on or

Fig. 2.15
Check Boxes

off. Selected options show a tick in the box against the option name, while incompatible options appear greyed out. If you want to see the adjacent Check boxes, use the **Tools, Options** command and select the View tab of the Word Options dialogue box.

To cancel a dialogue box, either click the **Cancel** button, or press the <Esc> key. Pressing the <Esc> key in succession, closes one dialogue box at a time, and eventually aborts the menu option.

# The Mouse Pointers

In Microsoft Word, as with all other graphical based programs, using a mouse makes many operations both easier and more fun to carry out.

Word 2002 makes use of the mouse pointers available in Windows, some of the most common of which are illustrated below. When Word is initially started up the first you will see is the hourglass, which turns into an upward pointing hollow arrow once the individual application screen appears on your display. Other shapes depend on the type of work you are doing at the time.

 The hourglass which displays when you are waiting while performing a function.

 The arrow which appears when the pointer is placed over menus, scrolling bars, and buttons.

I The I-beam which appears in normal text areas of the screen. For additional 'Click and Type' pointer shapes, see the table overleaf.

 The 4-headed arrow which appears when you choose to move a table, a chart area, or a frame.

↔       The double arrows which appear when over the border of a window, used to drag the side and alter the size of the window.

🖱       The Help hand which appears in the Help windows, and is used to access 'hypertext' type links, (with the <Ctrl> key depressed).

Word 2002, like other Windows packages, has additional mouse pointers which facilitate the execution of selected commands. Some of these have the following functions:

↓       The vertical pointer which appears when pointing over a column in a table or worksheet and used to select the column.

→       The horizontal pointer which appears when pointing at a row in a table or worksheet and used to select the row.

↖       The slanted arrow which appears when the pointer is placed in the selection bar area of text or a table.

↔‖↔     The vertical split arrow which appears when pointing over the area separating two columns and used to size a column.

≑       The horizontal split arrow which appears when pointing over the area separating two rows and used to size a row.

+       The cross which you drag to extend or fill a series.

✎       The draw pointer which appears when you are drawing freehand.

Word has a few additional mouse pointers to the ones above, but their shapes are mostly self-evident.

# Click and Type

With Word 2002, when in Print Layout and Web Layout views, you can quickly insert text, graphics, tables, or other items in a blank area of your document by using the 'Click and Type' facility. Just double-click in a blank area and the paragraph formatting to position the item is automatically applied.

What formatting Click and Type applies when you double-click depends on the 'zone' of the document you are in. As you move the pointer into a specific formatting zone the pointer shape indicates which formatting will be applied, as shown in our table below. For instance, if you double-click in the middle of a blank page entered text will be centred.

| I≣ | Align left | ≣I | Align right |
|---|---|---|---|
| I≣ | Centre | I≣ | Left indent |
| I≣ | Left text wrap | ≣I | Right text wrap |

If you don't see the Click and Type pointer shape, activate the facility using the **Tools**, **Options** command, then click the Edit tab and check the **Enable click and type** box. Then try moving the pointer around a blank Word screen to see how it changes. You will probably have to try this out a few times before you are completely happy with it.

# Getting Help in Word

No matter how experienced you are, there will always be times when you need help to find out how to do something in Word 2002. It is after all a very large and powerful package with a multitude of features. As in previous versions of Word the much maligned Office Assistant, or Clippy as he is called by Microsoft, is still available, but by default it is switched off. It is also possible to install Word 2002 without the Assistant, if the option is not selected in the Setup box we showed in Fig. 1.3. As we shall see, there are several ways to get help now.

## The Ask a Question Box

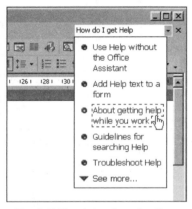

Fig. 2.16 The Ask a Question Box

To quickly access Help, you can use the Ask a Question box on the menu bar. You type a question in this box, as we show in Fig. 2.16, and press the Enter key.

A list of help topics is then displayed, as shown here. To see more topics, left-click the small triangle at the bottom of the list with the caption 'See more'. Once you select an option from the list and click on it, the Help system is opened and you should quickly be able to find the answers you need. In fact it works the same way as the Assistant, but without the constant 'distractions'.

It seems to be better to type a full question in the Ask a Question box, rather than just a keyword. The options presented can then be more relevant. When you use the feature several times, the previous questions can be accessed by clicking the down arrow to the right of the text box. The list is cleared whenever you exit Word though.

## The Office Assistant

The Office Assistant is turned off by default in this version of Word and may not even be installed unless you specifically request it. When activated, it first appears as we show on the left, and automatically provides Help topics and tips on tasks you perform as you work. To find out how it works, start Word and use the **Help**, **Show the Office Assistant** menu command. This should open Clippy. Now just click him with the left mouse button, to open the 'What would you like to do?' box, shown in Fig. 2.17.

Fig. 2.17
Using the Office Assistant

To get help you simply type your query here and click the **Search** button. From then on the procedure is the same as with the Ask a Question box.

If you like, you can customise the Assistant, and decide if you want it to automatically display tips, messages, and alerts, make sounds, move when it's in the way, and guess a Help topic that it thinks you

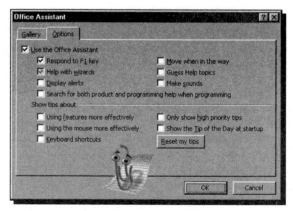

Fig. 2.18 The Office Assistant Options Box

may need. You can also switch it off once you have mastered a particular Office application, or cannot cope with its intrusions any more! All of these features are controlled from the box shown in Fig. 2.18 which is opened by clicking the **Options** button shown in Fig. 2.17.

To change the shape of your Office Assistant (there are eight shapes to choose from), either left-click the Gallery tab of the dialogue box shown in Fig. 2.18, or right-click the Office Assistant and select the **Choose Assistant** option from the displayed menu, as shown here in Fig. 2.19.

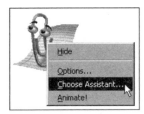

Fig. 2.19 Shortcut Menu

Either of these actions displays the following dialogue box (Fig. 2.20) in which you can select your preferred Assistant shape by left-clicking the **Next** button.

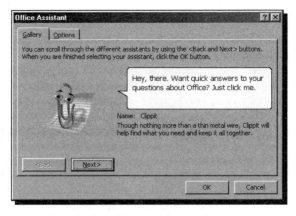

Fig. 2.20 The Office Assistant Gallery Box

The eight shapes of the available Assistants are shown in Fig. 2.21 on the next page. We find the Office Assistant's animated characters to be very clever and amusing, but must admit that like most people we prefer to work with the facility turned off. To do this, make sure the **Use the Office Assistant** option is not selected in the Options box shown in Fig. 2.18.

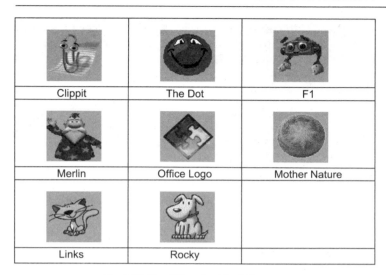

| Clippit | The Dot | F1 |
|---|---|---|
| Merlin | Office Logo | Mother Nature |
| Links | Rocky | |

Fig. 2.21 The Office Assistant Shapes

## The Main Help System

If you turn the Office Assistant completely off (as described on the last page) and press the **F1** function key, or click the **Help** toolbar button shown here, or use the **Help**, **Microsoft Word Help** menu command, Help will be accessed directly through the Help window. This is the way we prefer to use it.

When first opened, the Microsoft Word Help Center will be displayed in the right-hand pane as shown in Fig. 2.22 on the next page. This gives a quick way to get information on **What's New** with Word 2002, the **Microsoft Office Web Site** and about **Getting Help** itself. Each of these has a very colourful button you can press.

Below these is a listing of 'hypertext links' to some of the help topics Microsoft thought you were most likely to use first. Clicking any of these opens the relevant Help page, without you having to look for the item itself.

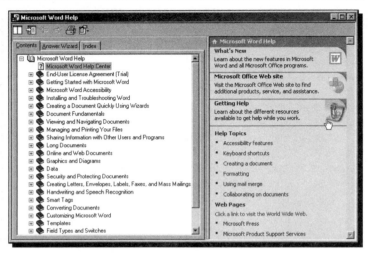

Fig. 2.22 Microsoft Word Help

As can be seen here, the left pane of the Help window has three tabbed sections.

Fig. 2.23 Help Contents List

The **Contents** tab of the Help screen opens up an impressive list of topics relating to the Word 2002 program. Clicking a '+' at the left of an item, or double-clicking a closed book icon, opens a sub-list; clicking a '—', or double-clicking an open book icon, will close it again. Clicking a list item, with the ▣ mark as shown, opens the help text in the right-hand pane.

To type a question in the Help window, you click the **Answer Wizard** tab. When you want to search for specific words or phrases, you click the **Index** tab.

For example, click the **Answer Wizard** tab, and type the text *How do I open a document* in the **What would you like to do?** text box. Then click the **Search** button and you should see something like the following.

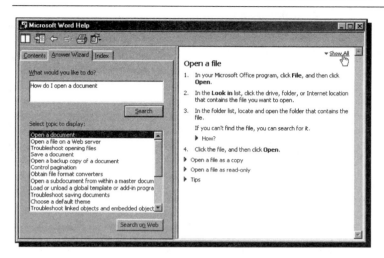

Fig. 2.24 Using the Help Answer Wizard

Clicking an item in the list of topics opens the relevant Help page in the right pane. A new feature with Office XP is that the Help pages are opened in an 'outline' view. Clicking a blue link item with a ▶ symbol to its left, opens up more detail. Whereas clicking the ▼ **Show All** link in the top-right corner will fully expand the page. This is very useful if you want to print or copy the Help information.

## The Help Toolbar

You can control the Help window with the six buttons on the toolbar, as follows:

**Auto Tile** - Tiles the Help window on the screen next to the main Word window.

**Hide** - Closes and re-opens the left half of the Help window, giving more room for the Help text.

**Back** - Opens the last Help page viewed in the current session list.

**Forward** - Opens the next Help page viewed in the current session list.

 **Print** - prints either the current page, or all of the topics in the selected heading.

 **Options** - gives a sub-menu of all the other toolbar options, as well as allowing you to hide the Help tabs.

The Word Help system is quite comprehensive but it is not always easy to find the information you are looking for. It sometimes pays to select the feature, or object, you want details on before accessing Help, you may then get exactly the right information straight off. Do spend some time here to learn, particularly what is new in Word. Other topics can always be explored later.

## ScreenTips

If you want to know what a menu command or button does, or if you want to know more about an option in a dialogue box, you can also get ScreenTips help. These can be accessed in three ways:

- For help with a menu command, toolbar icon, or a screen region, click **What's This?** on the **Help** menu, or <Shift + F1>, and then click the feature you want help on.

- In a dialogue box, click the Help icon 🖹 in the top right corner of the box, and then click the option.

- To see the name of a toolbar button, rest the pointer over the button and its name will appear.

## Help on the Internet

If all else fails, you can connect to several Microsoft Web sites with the **Help**, **Office on the Web** menu command. You must obviously have an Internet connection for this to work, though!

# 3

# Word Document Basics

When the program is first used, all Word's features default to those shown in Fig. 2.2. It is quite possible to use Word in this mode, without changing any main settings, but obviously it is possible to customise the package to your needs, as we shall see later.

## Entering Text

In order to illustrate some of Word's capabilities, you need to have a short text at hand. We suggest you type the memo below into a new document. At this stage, don't worry if the length of the lines below differ from those on your display.

As you type in text, any time you want to force a new line, or paragraph, just press <Enter>. While typing within a paragraph, Word sorts out line lengths automatically (known as 'word wrap'), without you having to press any keys to move to a new line.

MEMO TO PC USERS
Networked Computers
The microcomputers in the Data Processing room are a mixture of IBM compatible PCs with Pentium processors running at various speeds. They all have 3.5" floppy drives of 1.44MB capacity, and most also have CD-ROM drives. The PCs are connected to various printers via a network; the Laser printers available giving best output.

The computer you are using will have at least a 10.0GB capacity hard disc on which a number of software programs, including the latest version of Windows, have been installed. To make life easier, the hard disc is highly structured with each program installed in a separate folder.

# Moving Around a Document

You can move the cursor around a document with the normal direction keys, and with the key combinations listed below.

| *To move* | *Press* |
|---|---|
| Left one character | ← |
| Right one character | → |
| Up one line | ↑ |
| Down one line | ↓ |
| Left one word | Ctrl+← |
| Right one word | Ctrl+→ |
| To beginning of line | Home |
| To end of line | End |
| To paragraph beginning | Ctrl+↑ |
| To paragraph end | Ctrl+↓ |
| Up one screen | PgUp |
| Down one screen | PgDn |
| To top of previous page | Ctrl+PgUp |
| To top of next page | Ctrl+PgDn |
| To beginning of file | Ctrl+Home |
| To end of file | Ctrl+End |

Fig. 3.1 Page
Change Controls

To move to a specified page number in a multi-page document, either drag the vertical scroll bar up or down until the required page number is shown, as in Fig. 3.1, or use the **Edit**, **Go To** command (or <Ctrl+G>), as described on page 22.

To easily step from page to page you can also click the Previous Page ▲ and Next Page ▼ buttons, shown in Fig. 3.1.

Obviously, you need to become familiar with these methods of moving the cursor around a document, particularly if you spot an error in a document which needs to be corrected, which is the subject of the latter half of this chapter.

# Templates and Paragraph Styles

As we saw under the Formatting Bar section earlier, when you start Word for the first time, the Style box contains the word **Normal**. This means that all the text you have entered, at the moment, is shown in the Normal paragraph style which is one of the styles available in the NORMAL template. Every document produced by Word has to use a template, and NORMAL is the default. A template contains, both the document page settings and a set of formatting instructions which can be applied to text.

## Changing Paragraph Styles

To change the style of a paragraph, first open the Styles and Formatting Task Pane by clicking its toolbar button, as shown here. Place the cursor in the paragraph in question, say the title line and select the **Heading 1** style from the **Pick formatting to apply** list in the Task Pane. The selected paragraph reformats instantly in bold, and in Arial typeface of point size 16.

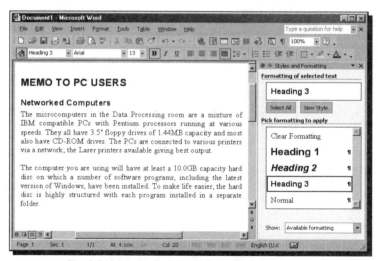

Fig. 3.2 Using the Styles and Formatting Task Pane

Now with the cursor in the second line of text, select **Heading 3** which reformats the line in Arial 13. Your memo should now look presentable, and be similar to Fig. 3.2 on the previous page.

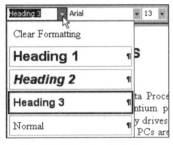

Fig. 3.3 Using the Style Box

The other way of setting these styles is from the Style box on the Word Formatting toolbar, as shown here in Fig. 3.3. This was the usual way in the previous version of Word, which did not have Task Panes.

If you try both methods you will find that in the long run the Task Pane method is better. You can carry out most, if not all, of your style format work from the Task Pane without having to resort to dialogue boxes. Microsoft have included Task Panes to make the features of Word more accessible.

# Document Screen Displays

Fig. 3.4 View Menu

Word provides four display views, **Normal**, **Web Layout**, **Print Layout**, and **Outline**, as well as the options to view your documents in a whole range of screen enlargements by selecting **Zoom**. You control all these viewing options with the **View** sub-menu, shown here, and when a document is displayed you can switch freely between them. When first loaded the screen displays in Print Layout view.

The main view options have the following effect, and can also be accessed by clicking the Views buttons on the left of the Status bar.

**Normal Layout**

A view that simplifies the layout of the page so that you can type, edit and format text quickly. In normal view, page boundaries, headers and footers, backgrounds, drawing objects, and pictures that do not have the **'In line with text'** wrapping style do not appear.

**Web Layout**

A view that optimises the layout of a document to make online reading easier. Use this layout view when you are creating a Web page or a document that is viewed on the screen. In Web layout view, you can see backgrounds, text is wrapped to fit the window, and graphics are positioned just as they are in a Web browser.

**Print Layout**

Provides a WYSIWYG (what you see is what you get) view of a document. The text displays in the typefaces and point sizes you specify, and with the selected attributes.

This view is useful for editing headers and footers, for adjusting margins, and for working with columns and drawing objects. All text boxes or frames, tables, graphics, headers, footers, and footnotes appear on the screen as they will in the final printout.

**Outline Layout**

Provides a collapsible view of a document, which enables you to see its organisation at a glance. You can display all the text in a file, or just the text that uses the paragraph styles you specify. Using this mode, allows you to quickly rearrange large sections of text. Some people like to create an outline of their document first, consisting of all the headings, then to sort out the document structure and finally fill in the text.

With large documents, you can create what is known as a master document by starting with an Outline View, and then designate headings in the outline as sub-documents. When you save the master document, Word assigns names to each sub-document based on the text you use in the outline headings.

**Document Map**

This view displays a separate pane with a list of document headings. You can quickly navigate through the document, when you click a heading Word jumps to that place in the document and displays the heading at the top of the window.

**Full Screen**

Selecting the **View, Full Screen** command, displays a clean, uncluttered screen; the Toolbars, Ruler, Scroll bars, and Status bar are removed. To return to the usual screen, click the **Close Full Screen** button on the icon which appears  at the bottom of your screen when in this mode.

**Zoom**

The **Zoom** command opens the Zoom dialogue box, in which you can change the screen viewing magnification factor from its default value of 100%.

# Changing Word's Default Options

## Modifying Margins

It is easy to change the standard page margins for your entire document from the cursor position onward, or for selected text (more about this later).

Select the **File, Page Setup** command, click the left mouse button on the **Margins** tab of the displayed dialogue box, shown in Fig. 3.5 below, and change any of the margin or gutter settings in the **Margins** boxes.

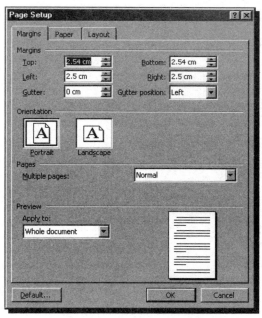

Fig. 3.5 Margins Sheet of the Page Setup Box

The **Preview** page at the bottom of the box shows how your changes will look on a real page. The orientation of the printed page is normally **Portrait** where text prints across the page width, but you can change this to **Landscape** which prints across the page length, if you prefer.

## Changing the Default Paper Settings

To change the default paper settings from those set during installation you do the following.

As before, select the **File, Page Setup** command, but click the **Paper** tab on the Page Setup dialogue box. Click the down-arrow against the **Paper size** box to reveal the list of available paper sizes, as shown in Fig. 3.6. Change the page size to your new choice.

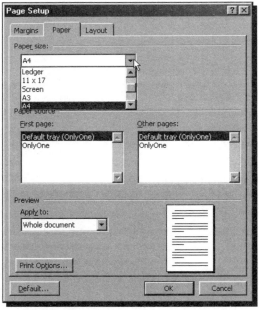

Fig. 3.6 Paper Sheet of the Page Setup Box

Any changes you can make to your document from the Page Setup dialogue box can be applied to either the whole document or to the rest of the document starting from the current position of the insertion pointer. To set this, click the down-arrow button against the **Apply to** box and choose from the drop-down list. To make any of the new settings you make 'permanent', press the **Default** button and confirm that you wish this change to affect all new documents based on the Normal template.

The Paper source section of the Page Setup box lets you set where your printer takes its paper from. You might have a printer that holds paper in trays, in which case you might want to specify that the **First page** (headed paper perhaps), should be taken from one tray, while **Other pages** should be taken from a different tray.

## Modifying the Page Layout

Clicking the last Page Setup tab displays the Layout box, part of which is shown here. From this dialogue box you can set options for headers and footers, section breaks, vertical alignment and whether to add line numbers or borders.

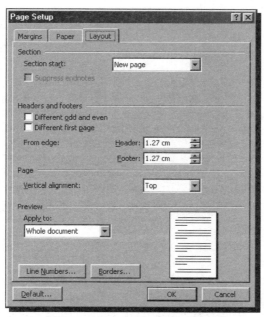

Fig. 3.7 Layout Sheet of the Page Setup Box

The default for **Section Start** is 'New Page' which allows the section to start at the top of the next page. Pressing the down arrow against this option, allows you to change this choice.

In the Headers and Footers section of the dialogue box, you can specify whether you want one header or footer for even-numbered pages and a different header or footer for odd-numbered pages. You can further specify if you want a different header or footer on the first page from the header or footer used for the rest of the document. Word aligns the top line with the 'Top' margin, but this can be changed with the **Vertical alignment** option.

## Changing Other Default Options

You can also change the other default options available to you in Word 2002, by selecting the **Tools, Options** command. This opens the Options dialogue box displayed in Fig. 3.8 below.

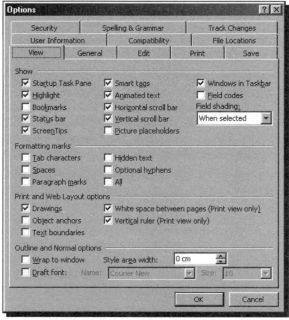

Fig. 3.8 The Word Options Dialogue Box

As can be seen, this box has eleven tabbed sheets which give you control of most of the program's settings.

You can, amongst other things, do the following:

- Specify the default **View** options. For example, you can select whether non-printing formatting characters, such as Tabs, Spaces, and Paragraph marks, are shown or not.

- Adjust the **General** Word settings, such as background re-pagination, display of the recently used file-list, and selection of units of measurement.

- Adjust the **Print** settings, such as allowing background printing, reverse print order, or choose to print comments with documents.

- Change the **Save** options, such as selecting to always create a backup copy of your work.

# Saving to a File

To save a document to disc, use either of the commands:

- **File, Save** (or click the **Save** toolbar button) which is used when a document has previously been saved to disc in a named file; using this command saves your work under the existing filename automatically without prompting you.

- **File, Save As** command which is used when you want to save your document with a different name from the one you gave it already.

Using the **File, Save As** command (or with the very first time you use the **File, Save** command when a document has no name), opens the dialogue box shown in Fig. 3.9 on the next page.

Note that the first 255 characters of the first paragraph of a new document are placed and highlighted in the **File name** field box, with the program waiting for you to over-type a new name.

Fig. 3.9 The File Save As Box

Any name you type must have less than 255 characters and will replace the existing name. Filenames cannot include any of the following keyboard characters: /, \, >, <, *, ?, ", |, :, or ;. Word adds the file extension **.doc** automatically and uses it to identify its documents.

You can select a drive other than the one displayed, by clicking the down arrow against the **Save in** text box at the top of the Save As dialogue box. You can also select a folder in which to save your work. The large buttons on the left of the box give rapid access to five possible saving locations. If you do not have a suitably named folder, then you can create one using the **Create New Folder** button, as shown below.

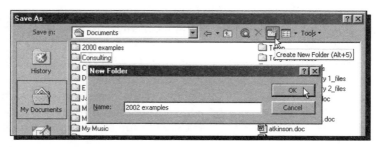

Fig. 3.10 Creating a New Folder

We used this facility to create a folder called **2002 examples** within the **Documents** folder. To save our work currently in memory, we selected this folder in the **Save in** field of the Save As dialogue box, then moved the cursor into the **File name** box, and typed **PC Users1**. We suggest you do the same.

By clicking the **Save as type** button at the bottom of the Save As dialogue box, you can save the Document Template, or the Text Only parts of your work, or you can save your document in a variety of 29 formats, including Rich Text, and several Web Page options.

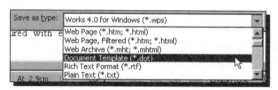

Fig. 3.11 Saving a Document as a Different File Type

## Selecting File Location

You can select where Word automatically looks for your document files when you first choose to open or save a document, by selecting the **Tools, Options** command, click the File Locations tab of the displayed Options dialogue box, (Fig. 3.8), and modify the location of the document files, as shown on the next page in Fig. 3.12.

As you can see, the default location of other types of files is also given in this dialogue box.

Microsoft suggests that you store documents, worksheets, presentations, databases, and other files you are currently working on, in the **My Documents** folder, which is easily accessed from the Desktop by clicking the special **Documents** button. This, of course, is a matter of preference, so we leave it to you to decide. We prefer to create sub-folders within **My Documents** to group our files more closely.

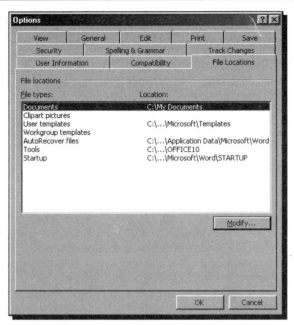

Fig. 3.12 Setting Word's File Locations

To change the default folder for any of the file types listed above, simply select the type and click the **Modify** button. This opens a dialogue box very similar to the Save As box for you to locate or even create the folder you want to select.

Fig. 3.13
Menu

While any of the file opening, saving and location dialogue boxes are open you can use them to generally manage your files and folders. You do this by right-clicking on the name of a file or folder you want to manipulate. A context sensitive menu is opened like ours in Fig. 3.13. All of these options may not be available on your system, but the common ones of Open, New, Print, Cut, Copy, Create Shortcut, Delete, Rename and Properties should always be there.

## Document Properties

A useful feature in Word is the facility to add document properties to every file by selecting the **File, Properties** command. A Properties box, as shown in Fig. 3.14 below, opens for you to type additional information about your document.

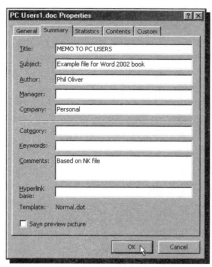

Fig. 3.14 The Document Properties Box

One of the most useful features in this box is the Statistics tabbed page.

| Statistic name | Value |
| --- | --- |
| Pages: | 1 |
| Paragraphs: | 4 |
| Lines: | 13 |
| Words: | 107 |
| Characters: | 538 |
| Characters (with spaces): | 641 |

Fig. 3.15
Document Statistics

As we show in Fig. 3.15, this gives a listing of the document statistics, including the number of pages, paragraphs, lines, words and even characters. Very useful for writing papers and reports, where the size is important.

To use this feature on a more regular basis, make sure that the **Prompt for document properties** box appears ticked on the Save tabbed sheet of the Options dialogue box (use the **Tools, Options** command and click the Save tab).

## Closing a Document

There are several ways to close a document in Word. Once you have saved it you can click its 'X' close button, or double-click on the **Document Control** button at the left end of the menu bar, or use the **File, Close** menu command.

If the document (or file) has changed since the last time it was saved, you will be given the option to save it before it is removed from memory.

If a document is not closed before a new document is opened, then both documents will be held in memory, but only one will be the current document. To find out which documents are held in memory, look at the Windows Taskbar, (see note below) or use the **Window** command to reveal the menu options shown in Fig. 3.16.

Fig. 3.16
Window Menu

In this case, the second document in the list is the current document, and to make another document the current one, either type the document number, or point at its name and click the left mouse button.

To close a document which is not the current document, use the **Window** command, make it current, and close it with one of the above methods.

**Note** - With Word 2002 it is now possible to limit what is shown on the Taskbar. By default all your open Word windows (or documents) will each have an entry on the Taskbar. But you can change this so that only the current, or active, document is shown there. This can be useful to save clutter if you have several programs open at the same time.

To do this, open the View tab sheet of the **Tools, Options** dialogue box, shown in Fig. 3.8, and uncheck the **Windows in Taskbar** option.

## Opening a Document

You can use the Open dialogue box in Word, shown in Fig. 3.17 below, to open documents that might be located in different locations. As we saw earlier, this is opened by clicking the **Open** toolbar button, or with the **File**, **Open** command, or the <Ctrl+O> keystrokes.

Fig. 3.17 The Open Dialogue Box

For example, you can open a document which might be on your computer's hard disc, or on a network drive that you have a connection to. To locate other drives and folders, simply click the **Up One Level** button pointed to in Fig. 3.18 below.

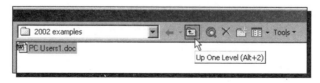

Fig. 3.18 The **Up One Level** Button

Having selected a drive, you can then select the folder within which your document was saved, select its filename and click the **Open** button on the dialogue box.

As in older versions of Word, the last few files you worked on are also listed at the bottom of the **File** menu, as shown in Fig. 3.19 below. Selecting one of these will reopen that file.

If you do not have any past files displayed, open the General tab sheet of the **Tools**, **Options** dialogue box, and make sure the **Recently used file list** option is checked. In the **entries** box next to it you can choose to have up to the last nine files listed. The default is four, which is probably plenty for most people.

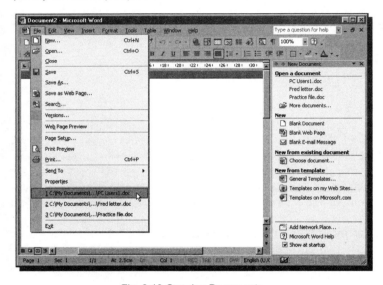

Fig. 3.19 Opening Documents

## The New Document Task Pane

The New document Task Pane, shown above, is another way of opening both new and recently used documents. If it is not open, simply use the **View**, **Task Pane** command.

The **Open a document** section at the top, lists the last few files you have used. Simply clicking on one will open it. The **More documents** option displays the Open dialogue box, seen in Fig. 3.17, for you to find and select an existing file to open.

The **New** section offers several options for opening new documents of different kinds. **Blank Document** opens a new empty document using the Normal template (the same as clicking the **New** toolbar button). **Blank Web Page** opens a blank page in Web layout view, for you to build a Web page. The **Blank E-mail Message** option lets you use Word to write an e-mail which you can then send using Outlook.

The **New from existing document** section is a very welcome new feature which lets you create a document based on the features of an existing one. You can click **Choose document** to open an existing file, maybe a letter with all your address and salutation details, and make any changes you want to it. When you click the **Save** toolbar button, however, the Save As dialogue box is opened with a new filename suggested. It was so easy before this to overwrite the old file accidentally during the saving process.

The last section **New from Template** lets you open a template to use for your document. Microsoft have produced 'hundreds' of templates for particular types of documents. These make it very easy for a 'newish' user to produce very professional documents. Once opened you just change the existing text to your own, print it and wait for the admiring comments - maybe. The **General Templates** option accesses those that came with Word, as shown in Fig. 3.20.

Fig. 3.20 Some of the Templates Available in Word

These templates are well worth exploring as you may save yourself an awful lot of work. In the example below we opened a new document with the Contemporary Letter template from the Letters & Faxes sheet.

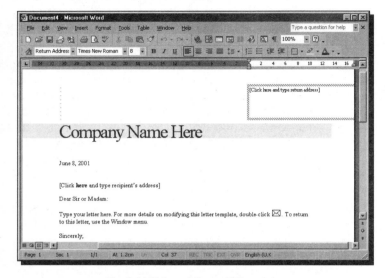

Fig. 3.21 Using a Microsoft Template

This letter has instructions in it that tell you what to customise and how. Once you have entered your name and address it is a good idea to save the document again, but as a template, so that you can use it again in the future. To do this, select Document Template in the **Save as type** box of the Save As dialogue box and rename the document. It will then be available in the General tabbed section of the Templates box, for you to use again and again.

The other two template options on the New Document Task Pane let you access templates from your own Web space, maybe a company intranet, or from Microsoft's own Web sites. That should keep you busy for a while!

As long as the **Show at startup** option is checked at the bottom of the pane, this list should always be available whenever you start up Word.

# 4

# Editing Word Documents

Microsoft have built some very clever editing facilities into Word 2002, and we will introduce some of them here. When you enter text you will notice that some basic errors are automatically corrected and that misspelled words are unobtrusively underlined in a red wavy line and ungrammatical phrases are similarly underlined in green.

## AutoCorrect

To demonstrate these, use the **File, New** command (or click ☐) to create a new file, and type the words 'teh computor is brukn', exactly as misspelled here.

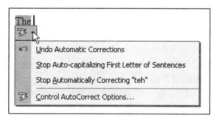

Fig. 4.1 The AutoCorrect Option Button

As soon as you press the space bar after entering the first 'word', it will be changed to 'The', as shown in Fig. 4.1. This is the **AutoCorrect** feature at work, which will automatically detect and correct typing errors, misspelled words, and incorrect capitalisation. If you agree with the change made, as in our example, all is well. If not, you can move the pointer over the corrected word until a blue box is shown below it. This changes to the **AutoCorrect Options** button when you point to it, and clicking it opens the menu shown above.

Selecting the first menu option **Undo Automatic Corrections** will cancel the correction for you. The other options give you control of how the feature works in the future, as we shall see a little later on.

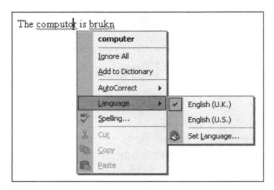

Fig. 4.2 Correcting Spelling Mistakes

What should appear on your screen is shown in Fig. 4.2, with the two misspelled words underlined in a red wavy line.

Right-clicking the first misspelled word allows you to correct it, as shown above. To do this, left-click the **Computer** menu option. You even have a choice of **Language** to use. This is possibly the most timesaving enhancement in editing misspelled words as you type.

During this process the status bar will indicate your 'state of play'. As shown in Fig. 4.3, the active language is displayed, English (UK) in our case. To the right of this, the small 'book' icon has three forms. In Fig. 4.3 it is ticked to indicate that spell checking is completed. If

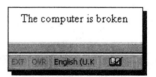

Fig. 4.3
The Status Bar

there are errors to correct, it has a red cross on it, and during the actual checking process it displays an active pencil as shown here to the left. If you double-click this icon when it displays a cross, the full spell and grammar checker is opened which will be discussed later in more detail.

If you really have a problem spelling particular words you can add them to the AutoCorrect list yourself. To do this, select the **AutoCorrect** option from the menu in Fig. 4.2 (or the **Tools**, **AutoCorrect Options** menu command) to open the AutoCorrect box shown in Fig. 4.4 on the next page.

Fig. 4.4 Controlling AutoCorrections

This dialogue box lets you control all of Word's automatic text, formatting and correction features, as well as the new Smart Tags feature we will encounter later on. Make sure the AutoCorrect tabbed sheet is active, as shown above, and have a good look at the ways you can control how it works for you. We suggest you scroll through the very long list of common misspellings at the bottom to see which ones will automatically be corrected.

In our example we have chosen to have the program always **Replace** the word 'computor' **With** the correct spelling of 'computer' as soon as we type the word. Clicking the **Add** button will add these to the AutoCorrect list.

The top fifteen options on the list are not corrections, but give you a rapid way to enter some common symbol characters by typing in a series of keyboard strokes. For example, if you type the three characters '(c)' AutoCorrect will change them to the copyright symbol '©'.

# Editing Text

Other editing could include deleting unwanted words or adding extra text in the document. All these operations are very easy to carry out. For small deletions, such as letters or words, the easiest method is to use the <Del> or <BkSp> keys.

With the <Del> key, position the cursor on the left of the first letter you want to delete and press <Del>. With the <BkSp> key, position the cursor immediately to the right of the character to be deleted and press <BkSp>. In both cases the rest of the line moves to the left to take up the space created by the deleting process.

Word processing is usually carried out in the insert mode. Any characters typed will be inserted at the cursor location (insertion point) and the following text will be pushed to the right, and down, to make room. To insert blank lines in your text, place the cursor at the beginning of the line where the blank line is needed and press <Enter>. To remove the blank line, position the cursor on it and press <Del>.

When larger scale editing is needed you have several alternatives. You could first 'select' the text to be altered, then use the **Cut, Copy** and **Paste** operations available in the **Edit** sub-menu, or more easily, click on their toolbar button alternatives shown here.

Another method of copying or moving text is to use the 'drag and drop' facility which requires you to highlight a word, grab it with the left mouse button depressed, and drop it in the required place in your text.

These operations will be discussed shortly in more detail.

# Selecting Text

The procedure in Word, as with most Windows based applications, is first to select the text to be altered before any operation, such as formatting or editing, can be carried out on it. Selected text is highlighted on the screen. This can be carried out in two main ways:

### A.  *Using the keyboard, to select:*

* A block of text.

  Position the cursor on the first character to be selected and hold down the <Shift> key while using the arrow keys to highlight the required text, then release the <Shift> key.

* From the present cursor position to the end of the line.

  Use <Shift+End>.

* From the present cursor position to the beginning of the line.

  Use <Shift+Home>.

* From the present cursor position to the end of the document.

  Use <Shift+Ctrl+End>.

* From the present cursor position to the beginning of the document.

  Use <Shift+Ctrl+Home>.

* Select the whole document.

  Use <Ctrl A>

### B.  With the mouse, to select:

- A block of text.

  Press down the left mouse button at the beginning of the block and while holding it pressed, drag the cursor across the block so that the desired text is highlighted, then release the mouse button.

- A word.

  Double-click within the word.

- A line.

  Place the mouse pointer in the selection bar (just to the left of the line, when it changes to an arrow ⇗) click once. For multiple lines, drag this pointer down.

- A sentence.

  Hold the <Ctrl> key down and click in the sentence.

- A paragraph.

  Place the mouse pointer in the selection bar and double-click (for multiple paragraphs, after selecting the first paragraph, drag the pointer in the selection bar) or triple-click in the paragraph.

- The whole document.

  Place the mouse pointer in the selection bar, hold the <Ctrl> key down and click once.

With Word 2002 you can now select non-contiguous text and graphics (ones that aren't next to each other), by selecting the first item you want, such as a word, sentence or paragraph, holding down the <Ctrl> key and selecting any other items from anywhere in the document. You can only select text, or graphics in this way, not both at the same time.

## Copying Blocks of Text

Once text has been selected it can be copied to another location in your present document, to another Word document, or to another Windows application, via the system clipboard. As with most of the editing and formatting operations there are several alternative ways of doing this, as follows:

- Use the **Edit, Copy** command sequence from the menu, to copy the selected text to the clipboard, moving the cursor to the start of where you want the copied text to be placed, and using the **Edit, Paste** command.

- Use the quick key combinations, <Ctrl+C> (or <Ctrl+Ins>) to copy and <Ctrl+V> (or <Shift+Ins>) to paste. This does not require the menu bar to be activated.

- Use the **Copy** and **Paste** Standard toolbar buttons; you can of course only use this method with a mouse.

 To copy the same text again to another location, or to any open document window or application, move the cursor to the new location and paste it there with any of these methods.

The above operations use the system clipboard which only holds the last item cut or copied. Microsoft Office XP comes with a new extra clipboard in which you can store 24 cut or copied items until they are needed. Each item is displayed as a thumbnail on the new Clipboard Task Pane as shown in Fig. 4.5 on the next page.

## The Clipboard Task Pane

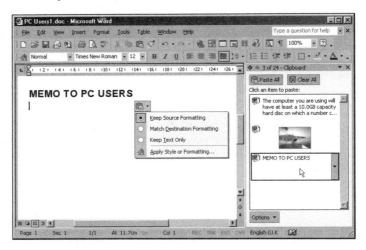

Fig. 4.5 Pasting from the Clipboard Task Pane

The Clipboard Task Pane opens automatically in Word when you cut or copy for the second time, otherwise you can open it with the **Edit**, **Office Clipboard** command.

Fig. 4.5 is actually a composite, showing the Clipboard Task Pane on the right with two text items and a picture. The bottom item (with the selection square around it) was clicked to paste the text at the insertion point location in the main document to the left.

This also shows another new Office XP feature, a Smart Tag button. By default, one of these is always placed just under newly pasted text in Word 2002. Clicking this button, as shown above, opens a menu which lets you control the style and formatting of the pasted text. If you don't want to make any formatting changes to the text, just carry on and the smart tag will 'go away'.

While the Clipboard Task Pane is active in any Office  program an icon like the one shown here is placed on the Windows task bar. This lets you easily access the pane, and also flags up how many items it contains.

## Moving Blocks of Text

Selected text can be moved to any location in the same document by either of the following:

- Using the **Edit, Cut,** command or <Ctrl+X> (or <Shift+Del>).

- Clicking the **Cut** toolbar button, shown here.

Next, move the cursor to the required new location and use any of the previously described procedures to paste the text where you want it.

The moved text will be placed at the cursor location and will force any existing text to make room for it. This operation can be cancelled by simply pressing <Esc>. Once moved, multiple copies of the same text can be produced by other **Paste** operations.

## Drag and Drop Operations

 Selected text, or graphics, can be **copied** by holding the <Ctrl> key depressed and dragging the mouse with the left button held down. The drag pointer is an arrow with two attached squares, as shown here - the vertical dotted line showing the point of insertion. The new text will insert itself where placed, even if the overstrike mode is in operation. Text copied by this method is not placed on the clipboard, so multiple copies are not possible as with other methods.

 Selected text can be **moved** by dragging the mouse with the left button held down. The drag pointer is an arrow with an attached square - the vertical dotted line showing the point of insertion.

## Deleting Blocks of Text

When text is 'cut' with the **Edit, Cut** command, or by clicking the **Cut** toolbar button, it is removed from the document, but placed on the clipboard. When the <Del> or <BkSp> keys are used, however, the text is not put on the clipboard.

# The Undo Command

As text is lost with the delete command, you should use it with caution, but if you do make a mistake all is not lost as long as you act promptly. The **Edit, Undo** command or <Ctrl+Z> reverses your most recent editing or formatting commands.

Fig. 4.6 The
Undo Cascade Menu

You can also use the **Undo** Standard toolbar button, shown here, to undo one of several editing or formatting mistakes (press the down arrow to the right of the button to see a list of your recent changes, as shown here).

Undo does not reverse any action once editing changes have been saved to file. Only editing done since the last save can be reversed.

# Finding and Changing Text

As in previous versions, Word 2002 allows you to search for specifically selected text, or character combinations with the **Find** or the **Replace** options on the **Edit** menu.

Using the **Find** option (<Ctrl+F>), will highlight each occurrence of the supplied text in turn so that you can carry out some action on it, such as change its font or appearance.

Using the **Replace** option (<Ctrl+H>), allows you to specify what replacement is to be automatically carried out. For example, in a long article you may decide to replace every occurrence of the word 'microcomputers' with the word 'PCs'.

To illustrate the **Replace** procedure, either select the option from the **Edit** sub-menu or use the quick key combination <Ctrl+H>. This opens the Find and Replace dialogue box shown on the next page with the **More** button clicked.

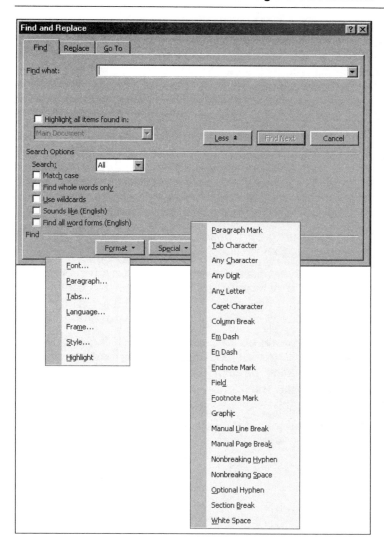

Fig. 4.7 A Composite of the Find and Replace Box

Towards the bottom of the dialogue box, there are five check boxes; the first two can be used to match the case of letters in the search string, and/or a whole word, while the last three are used for wildcard, 'sounds like' or 'word forms' matching.

The two buttons, **Format** and **Special**, situated at the bottom of the dialogue box, let you control how the search is carried out. The lists of available options, when either of these buttons is pressed, are displayed in Fig. 4.7. You will of course only see one or the other, but not both as shown here. You can force both the search and the replace operations to work with exact text attributes. For example, selecting:

- The **Font** option from the list under **Format**, displays a dialogue box in which you select a font (such as Arial, Times New Roman, etc.); a font-style (such as regular, bold, italic, etc.); an underline option (such as single, double, etc.); and special effects (such as strike-through, superscript, subscript, etc.).

- The **Paragraph** option, lets you control indentation, spacing (before and after), and alignment.

- The **Style** option, allows you to search for, or replace, different paragraph styles. This can be useful if you develop a new style and want to change all the text of another style in a document to use your preferred style.

Using the **Special** button, you can search for, and replace, various specified document marks, tabs, hard returns, etc., or a combination of both these and text, as listed in the previous screen dump.

Below we list only two of the many key combinations of special characters that could be typed into the **Find what** and **Replace with** boxes when the **Use wildcards** box is checked.

| *Type* | *To find or replace* |
|---|---|
| ? | Any single character within a pattern. For example, searching for nec?, will find <u>neck</u>, con<u>nect</u>, etc. |
| * | Any string of characters. For example, searching for c*r, will find such words as <u>cellar</u>, <u>chillier</u>, etc., also parts of words such as <u>character</u>, and combinations of words such as <u>connect, cellar</u>. |

A very useful new feature on the Find and Replace box is the **Highlight all items found in** option. If you tick this, your search will select all the matching words in your document at the same time. Any editing you then carry out will effect all of the selected text. This is a very rapid way of making global changes of font, size or style, etc.

## The Search Task Pane

 Clicking the **Search** toolbar button, shown here, opens the new Search Task Pane, shown in Fig. 4.8 on the right. This is really to help you locate particular files or text on your computer, but the **Find in this document** option at the bottom opens the Search and Replace dialogue box we have just looked at.

With the default **Basic Search** option this pane lets you search for files on your hard disc by name.

The **Advanced Search** option lets you search your files for particular text, particular authors, or for files with specific creation dates.

Fig. 4.8
The Search Task Pane

If you want more help on searching for files we suggest you click the **Search Tips** option, which opens the Word Help system at the relevant page.

# Page Breaks

The program automatically inserts a 'soft' page break in a document when a page of typed text is full. To force a

manual, or hard page break, either use the <Ctrl+Enter> keystrokes, or use the **Insert**, **Break** command and select **Page break** in the dialogue box, shown in Fig. 4.9.

Pressing **OK** places a series of dots across the page to indicate the page break (this can only be seen in Normal View), as shown in Fig. 4.10 below. If you are in Print Layout View, the second paragraph below appears

Fig. 4.9 Break Box

on the next page. To delete manual page breaks place the cursor on the line of dots, and press the <Del> key. In Print Layout View, place the cursor at the beginning of the second page and press the <BkSp> key.

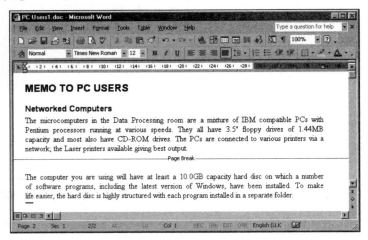

Fig. 4.10 A Hard Page Break in Normal View

Soft page breaks which are automatically entered by the program at the end of pages, cannot be deleted.

# Using the Spell Checker

The package has a very comprehensive spell checker which whenever it thinks it has found a misspelled word, underlines it with a red wavy line. To correct your document, right-click such words for alternatives, as we saw earlier.

 However, the spell checker can also be used in another way. To spell check your document, either click the **Spelling and Grammar** toolbar button, shown here, or use the **Tools**, **Spelling and Grammar** command (or **F7**) to open the dialogue box shown in Fig. 4.11 below.

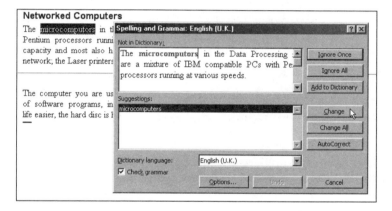

Fig. 4.11 Checking a Whole Document's Spelling

Make sure you are using the correct dictionary by checking in the **Dictionary language** box. With us this gave an enormous list of English, French and Spanish speaking country options. If you want to check a word or paragraph only, highlight it first. Once Word has found a misspelled word, you can either correct it in the **Not in Dictionary:** box, or select a word from the **Suggestions** list.

The main dictionary cannot be edited, but you can add specialised and personal dictionaries with the facility to customise and edit them. If you choose **Add**, the specified word is added to a custom dictionary.

# Using the Thesaurus

If you are not sure of the meaning of a word, or you want to use an alternative word in your document, then the thesaurus is an indispensable tool. To use the thesaurus, simply place the cursor on the word you want to look up and select the **Tools, Language, Thesaurus** command, or use the <Shift+F7> key combination. As long as the word is recognised, the following dialogue box will open.

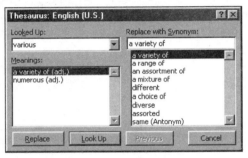

Fig. 4.12 The Thesaurus

This is a very powerful tool; you can see information about an item in the **Meanings** list, or you can look up a synonym in the **Replace with Synonym** list. To change the word in the **Looked Up** text box, select an offered word in either the **Meanings** or the **Replace with Synonym** list box, or type a word directly into the **Replace with Synonym** box, and press the **Replace** button.

You can use the thesaurus like a simple dictionary by typing any word into the **Replace with Synonym** box and clicking the **Look Up** button. If the word is recognised, lists of its meaning variations and synonyms will be displayed. Pressing the **Replace** button will place the word into the document.

A quick way to get a list of alternatives to a word in your document is to right-click it and select **Synonyms** from the drop-down menu. If you select one from the list it will replace the original word.

# The Grammar Checker

We find the Grammar Checker provided with Word to be much better than that of previous versions of the package. It does not have all the pre-set styles that we are sure were never used by anyone.

To illustrate using the Grammar Checker, open the **PC Users1** file and at the end of it type the following sentence which we know will cause some reaction from the grammar checker.

'Use the My Computer utility which Microsoft have spent much time and effort making as intuitive as possible.'

Straight away the Grammar Checker underlines the word 'have' with a green wavy line as shown below in Fig. 4.13.

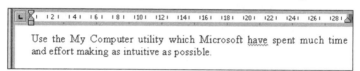

Fig. 4.13 Checking the Grammar of a Sentence

Right-clicking the wavy line opens a shortcut menu and choosing the **Grammar** option displays the following:

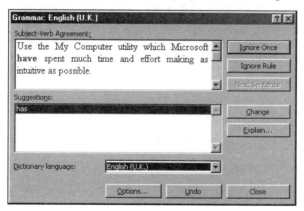

Fig. 4.14 The Grammar Checker

The Grammar Checker has picked up what is incorrect, as expected. No other errors were flagged up in this memo. Gone are the messages about 'Passive Verb Usage' which was the obsession of the Grammar Checker in some of the older versions of Word. If you want more information on the suggested changes, try clicking the new **Explain** button.

To see the Grammar Checker settings you use the **Tools, Options** command to open the Options dialogue box, and click the Spelling & Grammar tab, as shown in Fig. 4.15.

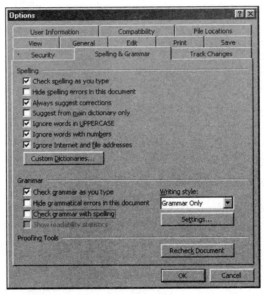

Fig. 4.15 The Spelling and Grammar Options

As you can see, you can to a certain extent customise the way the grammar checker works. For example, clicking the **Settings** button in the above dialogue box displays the Grammar Settings dialogue box shown in Fig. 4.16 on the next page.

Do spend some time with this dialogue box to find out all the available options before going on.

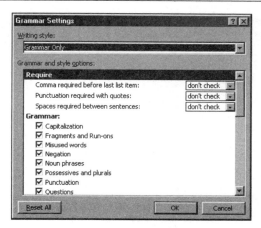

Fig. 4.16 The Grammar Settings Box

# Printing Documents

When Windows was first installed on your computer the printers you intend to use should have been selected, and the SETUP program should have installed the appropriate printer drivers. Before printing for the first time, it may be a good idea to check that your printer is in fact properly installed. To do this, click the Windows **Start** button (at the left end of the Task Bar) then select **Settings** and click the **Printers** menu option to open the Printers folder shown in Fig. 4.17 at the top of the next page.

Here, several printer drivers have been installed with Acrobat Distiller as the default, or active, printer (with its icon ticked) and an Epson Color printer which we often use, when we can afford the paper. In our case the Epson is configured to output to the printer via the USB port, yours may well be via the parallel port LPT1. These refer to the sockets at the back of your PC where you connect your printer. LPT1 is short for Line Printer No. and USB for Universal Serial Buffer.

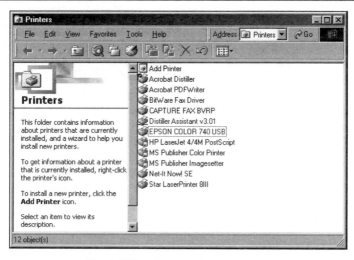

Fig. 4.17 The Windows Printers Folder

To see how a printer is configured (whether to print to a printer port or to a file), select it by clicking its button, use the **File, Properties** command and click the Details tab of the displayed dialogue box.

 Next, return to or reactivate Word and, if the document you want to print is not in memory, either click the **Open** button on the toolbar, or use the **File, Open** command, to display the Open dialogue box described in the previous chapter. Use this dialogue box to locate the file, or document, you want to print, which will be found on the drive and folder on which you saved it originally.

To print your document, do one of the following:

*   Click the **Print** button on the Standard toolbar, shown here, which prints the document using the default printer and current settings.

*   Use the **File, Print** command which opens the Print box, shown in Fig. 4.18 on the next page.

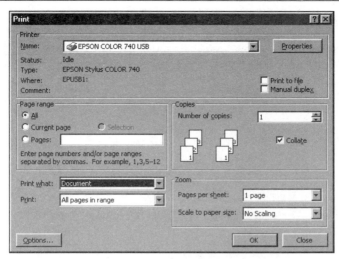

Fig. 4.18 The Print Dialogue Box

The settings in the Print dialogue box allow you to select the number of copies, and which pages, you want printed. You can also select to print the document, the summary information relating to that document, comments, styles, etc., in the **Print what** drop-down list.

You can even change the selected printer by clicking the down arrow against the **Name** box which displays the available printers on your system.

Clicking the **Properties** button on the Print dialogue box, displays the Properties dialogue box for the selected printer, shown here, which allows you to select the paper size, orientation needed, paper source, etc.

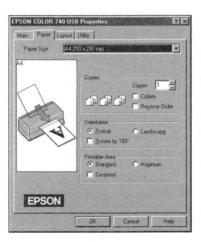

Fig. 4.19
A Printer Properties Box

The **Options** button on the Print dialogue box, gives you access to some more advanced print options, such as printing in reverse order, with or without comments, print hidden text or field codes, etc., as shown in Fig. 4.20 below.

Fig. 4.20 Some Advanced Print Options

Clicking the **OK** button on these various multilevel dialogue boxes, causes Word to accept your selections and return you to the previous level dialogue box, until the Print dialogue box is reached. Selecting **OK** on this first level dialogue box, sends print output from Word to your selection, either the printer connected to your computer, or to an encoded file on disc. Selecting **Cancel** or **Close** on any level dialogue box, aborts the selections made at that level.

Do remember that, whenever you change printers, the appearance of your document may change, as Word uses the fonts available with the newly selected printer. This can affect the line lengths, which in turn will affect both the tabulation and pagination of your document.

## Print Preview

Before printing your document to paper, click the **Print Preview** button on the Standard toolbar, or use the **File**, **Print Preview** command, to see what your print output will look like, and how much of your document will fit on your selected page size. This depends very much on the chosen font. In Fig. 4.21 below we show a preview of our example document PC Users1.doc.

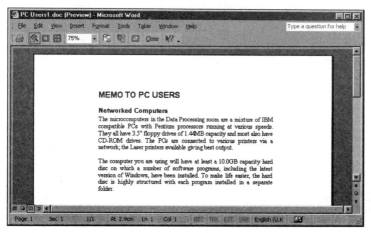

Fig. 4.21 A Print Preview of our Document

This view allows you to see the layout of the final printed page, which could save a few trees and equally important to you, a lot of frustration and wear and tear on your printer.

The print Preview window has its own toolbar with options for magnification and number of pages actually viewed. You can even edit your document, if you want to make any last minute changes. To print the document simply click the **Print** button, or to return to your working document from a print preview display, click the **Close** button.

Other enhancements of your document, such as selection of fonts, formatting of text, and pagination, will be discussed in the next chapter.

# 5

---

# Formatting Word Documents

Formatting involves the appearance of individual words or even characters, the line spacing and alignment of paragraphs, and the overall page layout of the entire document. These functions are carried out in Word in several different ways.

Primary page layout is included in a document's Template and text formatting in a Template's styles. Within any document, however, you can override Paragraph Style formats by applying text formatting and enhancements manually to selected text. To immediately cancel manual formatting, select the text and use the **Edit, Undo** command, or (<Ctrl+Z>). The selected text reverts to its original format. In the long term, you can cancel manual formatting by selecting the text and using the <Shift+Ctrl+N> key stroke. The text then reverts to its style format.

## Formatting Text

If you use TrueType fonts, which are automatically installed when you set up Windows, Word uses the same font to display text on the screen and to print on paper. The screen fonts provide a very close approximation of printed characters. TrueType font names are preceded by Tr in the Font box on the Formatting Bar.

If you use non-TrueType fonts, then use a screen font that matches your printer font. If a matching font is not available, or if your printer driver does not provide screen font information, Windows chooses the screen font that most closely resembles the printer font.

Originally, the title and subtitle of the **PC Users1** memo, were selected from the default Normal style as 'Heading 1' and 'Heading 3', which were in the 16 and 13 point size Arial typeface, respectively, while the main text was typed in 10 point size Times New Roman.

To change this memo into what appears on the screen dump displayed below, first select the title of the memo and format it to italics, 18 point size Arial and centre it between the margins, then select the subtitle and format it to 14 point size Arial. Both title and subtitle are in bold as part of the definition of their respective paragraph style. Finally select each paragraph of the main body of the memo in turn, and format it to 12 point size Times New Roman. Notice in each case that the Style details in the Style box on the Formatting toolbar is changed to show the manual formatting that was added. This shows as 'Normal + 12pt' in Fig. 5.1 below.

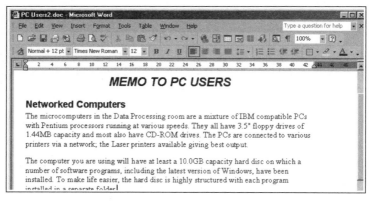

Fig. 5.1 The Re-formatted PC Users Memo

All of this formatting can be achieved by using the buttons on the Formatting toolbar (see also the section entitled 'Paragraph Alignment'). Save the result under the new filename **PC Users2**, using the **File, Save As** command.

In all our screen dumps so far we show the Formatting toolbar moved from its default position (to the right of the Standard toolbar) to just below it. Although this takes up more screen space, we have done this to show more buttons on both the toolbars.

## Moving Toolbars

As we have seen, the default buttons appearing on the two toolbars below the Menu Bar have distinctive functions. By default, the one to the left is the Standard toolbar, while the one to the right is the Formatting toolbar. Each of these two toolbars is preceded by a vertical handle. Moving the mouse pointer onto such a handle, changes it into a four-headed 'moving' pointer, as shown here in Fig. 5.2. With the left mouse button held down you can then drag the toolbar around the screen.

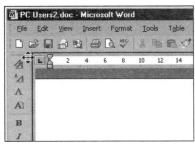

Fig. 5.2 Moving a Toolbar

As we show here, it is possible to move toolbars to any part of the screen, and also change the buttons contained in each (see Fig. 2.3 on page 20). Through this book we have moved the Formatting bar and placed it below the Standard toolbar. This gives a good compromise between screen space taken up by the bars and the number of buttons displayed.

To see additional sets of toolbars, use the **View**, **Toolbars** command to open up a menu of options, as shown in our previous Fig. 2.11 on page 30. You can toggle these on and off by clicking on their names. Be careful, however, how many of these you activate, as they take valuable screen space.

## Text Enhancements

In Word all manual formatting, including the selection of font, point size, style (bold, italic, highlight, strike-through, hidden and capitals), colour, super/subscript, spacing and various underlines, are carried out by first selecting the text and then executing the formatting command.

With some actions the easiest way of activating the formatting commands is from the Formatting Bar. With others you have to use the **Format**, **Font** menu command, and select options from the dialogue box below.

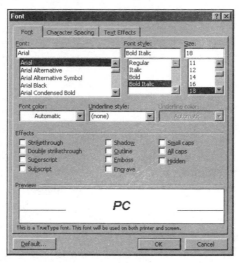

Fig. 5.3 The Font Box

Yet another method is by using quick keys, some of which are listed below:

| *To Format* | *Type* |
|-------------|--------|
| Bold | Ctrl+B |
| Italic | Ctrl+I |
| Underline | Ctrl+U |
| Word underline | Ctrl+Shift+W |

There are quick keys to do almost anything, but the ones listed here are the most useful and the easiest to remember.

## Paragraph Alignment

Word defines a paragraph, as any text which is followed by a paragraph mark, which is created by pressing the <Enter> key. So single line titles, as well as sections of long typed text, can form paragraphs.

 The paragraph symbol, shown here, is only visible in your text if you have selected the **Show/Hide ¶** button from the Standard toolbar, or used <Ctrl+*>.

Word allows you to align a paragraph at the left margin (the default), at the right margin, centred between both margins, or justified between both margins. As with most operations there are several ways to perform alignment in Word. Three such methods are:

- Using buttons on the **Formatting Bar**.

- Using keyboard short cuts.

- Using the **Format, Paragraph** menu command.

The table below describes the buttons on the Formatting bar and their keystroke shortcuts.

| Buttons on Formatting Bar | Paragraph Alignment | Keystrokes |
|---|---|---|
| ≣ | Left | <Ctrl+L> |
| ≣ | Centred | <Ctrl+E> |
| ≣ | Right | <Ctrl+R> |
| ≣ | Justified | <Ctrl+J> |

Fig. 5.4 below shows the dialogue box resulting from using the **Format**, **Paragraph** command in which you can specify any **Left**, **Right**, or **Special** indentation required.

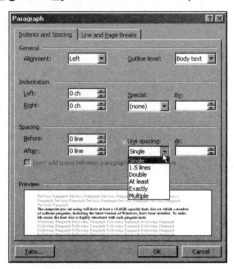

Fig. 5.4 The Paragraph Box

## Paragraph Spacing

The settings in this box will affect the current paragraph (with the insertion point in it), or any selected paragraphs. The above Paragraph dialogue box can also be used to set your paragraph line spacing to single-line, 1½-line, or double-line spacing. You can even set the spacing to any value you want by using the **At Least** option, as shown on the above screen dump, then specify what interval you want.

The available shortcut keys for paragraph spacing are as follows:

| To Format | Type |
|---|---|
| Single-spaced lines | Ctrl+1 |
| One-and-a-half-spaced lines | Ctrl+5 |
| Double-spaced lines | Ctrl+2 |

Whichever of the above methods is used, formatting can take place either before or after the text is entered. If formatting is selected first, then text will type in the chosen format until a further formatting command is given. If, on the other hand, you choose to enter text and then format it afterwards, you must first select the text to be formatted, then activate the formatting.

Word gives you the choice of 5 units to work with, inches, centimetres, millimetres, points or picas. These can be selected by using the **Tools**, **Options** command, choosing

the **General** tab of the displayed Options dialogue box, and clicking the down arrow against the **Measurement units** list box, shown open here, which is to be found at the bottom of the dialogue box. We have selected to work in the default centimetres.

## Indenting Text

Most documents will require some form of paragraph indenting. An indent is the space between the margin and the edge of the text in the paragraph. When an indent is set (on the left or right side of the page), any justification on that side of the page sets at the indent, not the page border.

To illustrate indentation, open the file **PC Users2**, select the first paragraph, and then choose the **Format**, **Paragraph** command. In the **Indentation** field, select 2.5 cm for both **Left** and **Right**, as shown on the next page. On clicking **OK**, the first selected paragraph is displayed indented. Our screen dump shows the result of the indentation as well as the settings on the Paragraph dialogue box which caused it.

You can also use the Formatting toolbar buttons, shown below, to decrease or increase the indent of selected text.

    Use this button to decrease indent.

    Use this button to increase indent.

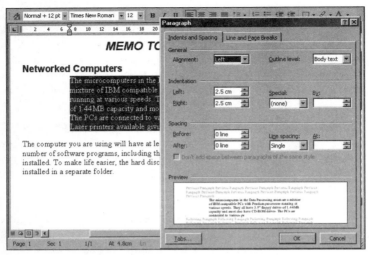

Fig. 5.5 Setting Paragraph Indentation

The **Indentation** option in the Paragraph dialogue box, can be used to create 'hanging' indents, where all the lines in a paragraph, including any text on the first line that follows a tab, are indented by a specified amount. This is often used in lists to emphasise certain points.

To illustrate the method, use the **PC Users1** file and add at the end of it the text shown below. After you have typed the text in, save the enlarged memo as **PC Users3**, before going on with formatting the new text.

---

In Windows you can work with files in three different ways:

Name Description

My Computer Use the My Computer utility which Microsoft has spent much time and effort making as intuitive as possible.

Explorer Use the Windows Explorer, a much-improved version of the older File Manager.

MS-DOS Use an MS-DOS Prompt window if you prefer to and are an expert with the DOS commands.

---

Saving the work at this stage is done as a precaution in case anything goes wrong with the formatting - it is sometimes much easier to reload a saved file, than it is to try to unscramble a wrongly formatted document!

Next, highlight the last 4 paragraphs above, use the **Format**, **Paragraph** command, and select 'Hanging' under **Special** and 3 cm under **By**. On clicking the **OK** button, the text formats as shown in the composite screen dump below, but it is still highlighted. To remove the highlighting, click the mouse button anywhere on the page. The second and following lines of the selected paragraphs, should be indented 3 cm from the left margin.

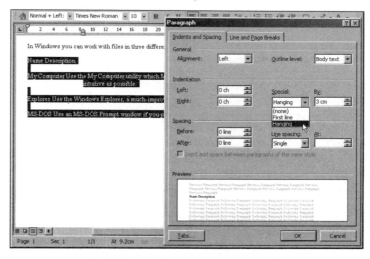

Fig. 5.6 Setting Hanging Indents Manually

This is still not very inspiring, so to complete the effect we will edit the first lines of each paragraph as follows:

Place the cursor in front of the word 'Description' and press the <Tab> key once. This places the start of the word in the same column as the indented text of the other paragraphs. To complete the effect place tabs before the words 'Use' in the next three paragraphs, until your hanging indents are correct, as shown on the next page.

In Windows you can work with files in three different ways:

| Name | Description |
|------|-------------|
| My Computer | Use the My Computer utility which Microsoft have spent much time and effort making as intuitive as possible. |
| Explorer | Use the Windows Explorer, a much-improved version of the older File Manager. |
| MS-DOS | Use an MS-DOS Prompt window if you prefer to and are an expert with the DOS commands. |

This may seem like a complicated rigmarole to go through each time you want the hanging indent effect, but with Word you will eventually set up all your indents, etc., as styles in templates. Then all you do is click in a paragraph to produce them.

## Adding a Drop Capital

Another text feature that you may want to use at times is to make the first letter of a paragraph a large dropped initial capital letter, as shown here.

With Word that is ridiculously easy. Just place the insertion point at the beginning of the existing paragraph and action the **Format**, **Drop Cap** menu command. This opens the Drop Cap dialogue box, shown in our composite Fig. 5.7. As is often the case, this gives the settings needed to produce the result shown. You would not normally see them both together.

You can choose between **Dropped** and **In margin** for the position of the initial capital letter, change the **Font** (as we have done) and select how many **Lines to drop**.

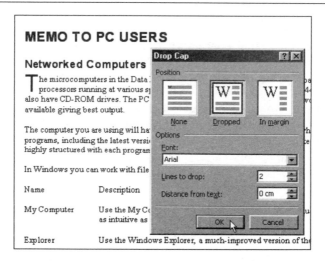

Fig. 5.7 Setting a Dropped Capital Letter

The new first letter is actually a graphic image now. To remove the effect if you decide you don't want it, select the image by clicking it, open the dialogue box with the **Format, Drop Cap** command and select **None**.

 When you finish formatting the document, save it under its current filename either with the **File, Save** command (<Ctrl+S>), or by clicking the **Save** button. This command does not display a dialogue box, so you use it when you do not need to make any changes during the saving operation.

## Inserting Bullets

Bullets are small characters you can insert, anywhere you like, in the text of your document to improve visual impact. In Word there are several choices for displaying lists with bullets or numbers. As well as the two Formatting toolbar buttons, others are made available through the **Format, Bullets and Numbering** command, which displays the following dialogue box.

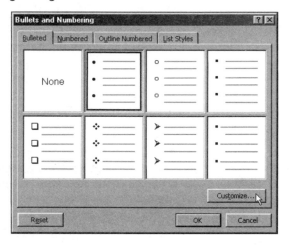

Fig. 5.8 Setting Bullets and Numbering Styles

You can select any of the bullets shown here, or you could click the **Customize** button to change the shape, font and size of the bullet, choose a character, and set the indentation in the Customize Bulleted List box shown on the left in Fig. 5.9.

Further, by pressing the **Picture** button on the Customized Bulleted List dialogue box you can select from an enormous number of bullet pictures, as shown on the right of Fig. 5.8. If none of these images suit, you can even **Import** a graphic image yourself to use as bullets. Very comprehensive.

If you select the **Numbered** or **Outline Numbered** tabs, shown in Fig. 5.8, similar dialogue boxes are displayed, giving you a choice of several numbering or outline (multilevel) systems.

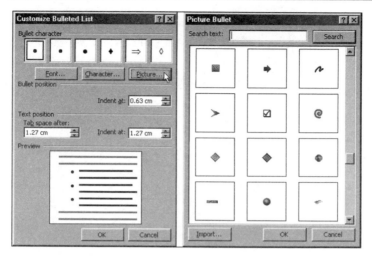

Fig. 5.9 Choosing Custom Bullet Pictures

Once inserted, you can copy, move or cut a bulleted paragraph in the same way as any other text. However, you can not delete a bullet with the <BkSp> or <Del> keys. To do  this, you need to place the insertion point in the line and click the **Bullets** toolbar button, shown here. Once you have set up a customised bullet, clicking this button in a paragraph will use it.

## Inserting Date and Time

You can insert today's date, the date the current document was created or was last revised, or a date or time that reflects the current system date and time into a document. Therefore, the date can be a date that changes, or a date that always stays the same. In either case, the date is inserted in a date field.

To insert a date field in your document, place the cursor where you want to insert the date, select the **Insert**, **Date and Time** command and choose one of the displayed date formats which suits you from the dialogue box shown in Fig. 5.10 on the next page.

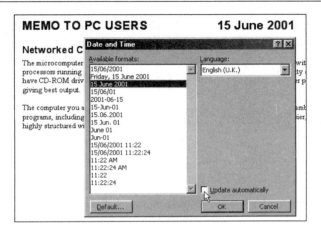

Fig. 5.10 Inserting Dates and Times in a Document

Highlighting '15 June, 2001' (or whatever date is current), and pressing **OK**, inserts the date in your document at the chosen position.

As before, the above screen is a composite of the operation required and the result of that operation.

If you save a document with a date field in it and you open it a few days later, the date shown on it will be the original date the document was created. Most of the time this will probably be what you want, but should you want the displayed date to always update to the current date whenever the document is opened, check the **Update automatically** box, pointed to in Fig. 5.10, and then click the **OK** button.

You may have noticed that many of Word's dialogue boxes have a **Default** button on them, as above. If you click this button you will make the settings active in the box at the time the default ones in any future documents opened with the Normal template. In our case the date would always be presented in the above format.

## Comments and Tracked Changes

Another powerful feature of Word is the facility to add comments and to track changes made to a document. Comments are notes, or annotations, that an author or reviewer adds to a document and in Word 2002 they are displayed in balloons in the margin of the document or in the Reviewing Pane, as shown in Fig. 5.11 below. A tracked change is a mark that shows where a deletion, insertion, or other editing change has been made in a document. To quickly display or hide tracked changes or comments (known as mark-up) use the **View**, **Markup** menu command.

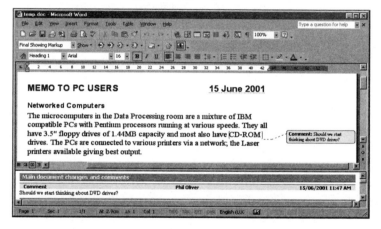

Fig. 5.11 A Comment in a Document with the Reviewing Pane Open

To add a comment, place the pointer in the correct location, use the **Insert**, **Comment** command, and type the comment into the balloon that opens. If the Reviewing toolbar shown above is hidden, simply right-click any toolbar, and then click Reviewing on the shortcut menu. To open the reviewing pane, as shown above, use the **Show**, **Reviewing Pane** command from the Reviewing toolbar.

You can print a document with markup to keep a record of any changes made. If you want to see comments and tracked changes in balloons you must be in Print Layout or Web Layout view.

# Formatting with Page Tabs

You can format text in columns by using tab stops. Word 2002 has default left tab stops every 3 ch from the left margin. We do not know what dimension the 'ch' is but the default tabs line up almost exactly at the old 1.27 cm intervals. By default the symbol for a left tab appears in the tab type button at left edge of the ruler as shown in Fig 5.12 below.

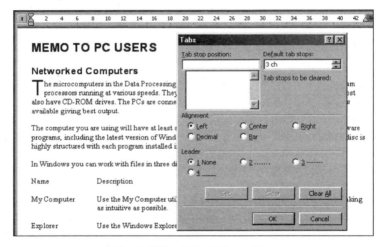

Fig. 5.12 The Tabs Dialogue Box

To set tabs, use either the **Format**, **Tabs** command which opens the Tabs dialogue box shown above, or click on the tab type button (which cycles through the available tab stops) until the type you want is showing and then click the required position on the lower half of the ruler. To remove an added tab, just drag it off the ruler.

To clear the ruler of tab settings press the **Clear All** button in the Tabs dialogue box. When you set a tab stop on the ruler, all default tab stops to the left of the one you are setting are removed. Tab stops apply either to the paragraph containing the cursor, or to any selected paragraphs.

The tab stop types available have the following functions:

| *Button* | *Name* | *Effect* |
|---|---|---|
| **L** | **Left** | Left aligns text after the tab stop. |
| **⊥** | **Centre** | Centres text on tab stop. |
| **⅃** | **Right** | Right aligns text after the tab stop. |
| **⅃•** | **Decimal** | Aligns decimal point with tab stop. |
| **I** | **Bar** | Inserts a vertical line at the tab stop |

The tab type button actually cycles through two more types, first line indent and hanging indent. This gives you a quick way of adding these indents to the ruler.

If you want tabular text to be separated by characters instead of by spaces, select one of the three available characters from the **Leader** box in the Tabs dialogue box. The options are none (the default), dotted, dashed, or underline. The Contents pages of this book are set with right tabs and dotted leader characters.

**Note:** As all paragraph formatting, such as tab stops, is placed at the end of a paragraph, if you want to carry the formatting of the current paragraph to the next, press <Enter>. If you don't want formatting to carry on, press the down arrow key instead.

# Formatting with Styles

We saw earlier on page 45, how you can format your work using Paragraph Styles, but we confined ourselves to using the default **Normal** styles only. In this section we will get to grips with how to create, modify, use, and manage styles.

As mentioned previously, a Paragraph Style is a set of formatting instructions which you save so that you can use it repeatedly within a document or in different documents. A collection of Paragraph Styles can be placed in a Template which could be appropriate for, say, all your memos, so it can be used to preserve uniformity. It maintains consistency and saves time by not having to format each paragraph individually.

Further, should you decide to change a style, all the paragraphs associated with that style reformat automatically. Finally, if you want to provide a pattern for shaping a final document, then you use what is known as a Template. All documents which have not been assigned a document template, use the **Normal.dot** global template, by default.

## Paragraph Styles

Paragraph Styles contain paragraph and character formats and a name can be attached to these formatting instructions. From then on, applying the style name is the same as formatting that paragraph with the same instructions.

With Word 2002 you create your styles by example using the new Styles and Formatting Task Pane, as we show in Fig. 5.13 on the next page.

***Creating a New Paragraph Style***: Previously, we spent some time manually creating some hanging indents in the last few paragraphs of the **PC Users3** document. Open that document and display the Styles and Formatting Task Pane by clicking its toolbar button, as shown here. Place the insertion pointer in one of the previously created hanging indent paragraphs, say, in the 'Name Description' line.

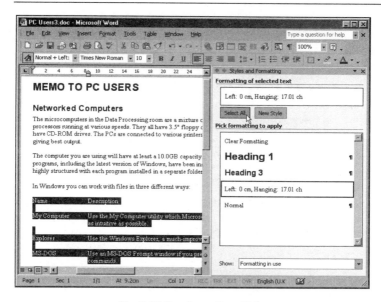

Fig. 5.13 Creating a New Style

Notice that the selected item in the **Pick formatting to apply**
list in the Task Pane has a rectangular selection marker
around it. This in fact represents an unnamed style with the

formatting we used to
create the hanging
indents. If you click the
**Select All** button in the
Task Pane all of our
paragraphs with this
formatting are highlighted
in the main document.

Next click the **New
Style** button in the Task
Pane to open the New
Style box shown in Fig.
5.14. Type the new style
name you want to create
in the **Name** text box,
say, 'Hanging Indent'.

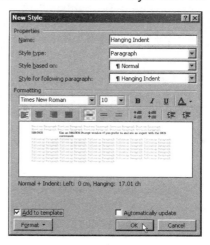

Fig. 5.14 The New Style Box

Lastly select the **Add to template** option at the bottom of the box and click **OK** to accept your changes.

Finally, one by one, highlight the other three paragraphs with hanging indents and change their style to the new 'Hanging Indent', by clicking the mouse in the **Style box** button on the Formatting toolbar and selecting the new style from the displayed list, as shown in Fig. 5.15 below.

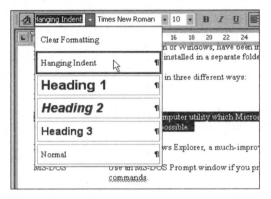

Fig. 5.15 Our New Style in Action

It would have been nice if this last step could be carried out in the Styles and Formatting Task Pane, but the older Style box still seems to be necessary. Once this is done, however, our new style functions exactly the same in the Task Pane as the other ones.

Save the result as **PC Users4**, and make yourself a cup of coffee, or chocolate, or whatever turns you on.

You could also have a look at Word's built-in styles by selecting **Style Gallery** from the **Format, Theme** menu. There are over sixty available styles, one of which might suit your type of document. Try them with the **PC Users4** file open, as it reformats your document on a viewing pane. Some of them may need installing though, but it will carry this out for you without too much trouble.

# Document Templates

A document template provides the overall pattern of your final document. It can contain:

- Styles to control your paragraph and formats.

- Page set-up options.

- Boilerplate text, which is text that remains the same in every document.

- AutoText, which is standard text and graphics that you could insert in a document by typing the name of the AutoText entry.

- Macros, which are programs that can change the menus and key assignments to comply with the type of document you are creating.

- Customised shortcuts, toolbars and menus.

If you don't assign a template to a document, then the default **Normal.dot** template is used by Word. To create a new document template, you either modify an existing one, create one from scratch, or create one based on the formatting of an existing document.

## Creating a Document Template

To illustrate the last point above, we will create a simple document template, which we will call **PC User**, based on the formatting of the **PC Users4** document. But first, make sure you have defined the 'Hanging Indent' style as explained earlier.

To create a template based on an existing document do the following:

- Open the existing document.

- Select the **File, Save As** command which displays the Save As dialogue box, shown in Fig. 5.16 overleaf.

- In the **Save as type** box, select Document Template.

Fig. 5.16 Saving a Document as a Template

- In the **Save in** box, use the Templates folder which should have opened for you.

- In the **File name** box, type the name of the new template (PC User in our example).

- Press the **Save** button, which opens the template file **PC User.dot** in the Word working area.

- Add the text and graphics you want to appear in all new documents that you base on this template, and *delete* any items (including text) you do not want to appear. In our example, we deleted everything in the document, bar the heading, and added the words 'PC User Group' using **Insert, Picture, WordArt**, to obtain:

Fig. 5.17 Artwork and Text in our New Template

- Click the **Save** button on the Standard toolbar, and close the document.

To use the new template, do the following:

- Use the **File**, **New** command which opens the New Document Task Pane. Select **General Templates** from the **New from template** section of the pane. The General tabbed sheet of the Templates box is opened, as shown in Fig. 5.18 below.

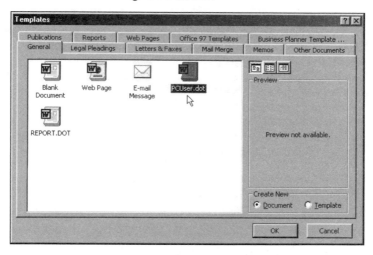

Fig. 5.18 The General Templates Including Our New One

- Select the name of the template you want to use from the displayed list. This would be PCUser.dot in our case.

- Make sure that the radio button **Document** is selected, and click the **OK** button.

The new document will be using the selected template.

Templates can also contain Macros as well as AutoText; macros allow you to automate Word keystroke actions only, while AutoText speeds up the addition of boilerplate text and graphics into your document. However, the design of these features is beyond the scope of this book.

Don't forget that Word has a series of built-in templates to suit 'every occasion' as we touched on in page 61.

# The Default Character Format

As we have seen, for all new documents Word uses the Times New Roman type font with a 12 points size as the default for the Normal style, which is contained in the Normal template. If the majority of your work demands some different font style or size, then you can change these defaults.

To change the default character formatting, use the **Format**, **Font** command, select the new defaults you want to use, and press the **Default** button, as shown in Fig. 5.19.

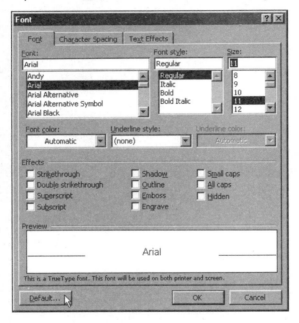

Fig. 5.19 Setting a New Default Font

A warning box opens to make sure you really know what you are about to do. Pressing the **Yes** button, changes the default character settings for this and all subsequent new documents using the Normal template, but does not change already existing ones. Pressing **No** aborts the operation.

# Special Characters and Symbols

Word 2002 has a redesigned Symbol dialogue box from which you can select characters and symbols and insert them into your document using the **Insert, Symbol** command. This is shown in Fig. 5.20 below.

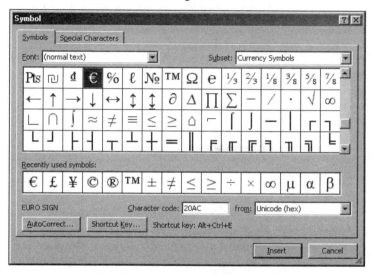

Fig. 5.20 The New Symbol Dialogue Box

You should be able to find just about any symbol you require in the (normal text) font displayed. But if not, pressing the down-arrow button next to the **Font** box, will reveal the other available character sets. If you double-click the left mouse button on a character, it transfers it to your document at the insertion point.

Microsoft have made it easier to find symbols by grouping them into sets. Clicking the **Subset** button opens a drop-down menu for you to quickly move between them.

The **AutoCorrect** button opens the box shown in Fig. 4.4 so that you can insert any of the symbols in the **Replace text as you type** section.

## Inserting Other Special Characters

You can include other special characters in a document, such as optional hyphens, which remain invisible until they are needed to hyphenate a word at the end of a line; non-breaking hyphens, which prevent unwanted hyphenation; non-breaking spaces, which prevent two words from splitting at the end of a line; or opening and closing single quotes.

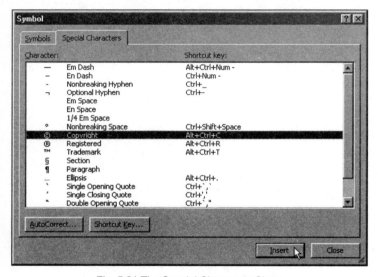

Fig. 5.21 The Special Characters Sheet

There are two ways to insert these special characters in your document. One is to click the **Special Characters** tab of the Symbol dialogue box which reveals a long list of these special characters, as shown in Fig. 5.21 above. You then select one of them and click the **Insert** button.

The other way is to use the shortcut key combinations listed above, which does not require you to open the dialogue box. But you do have to remember them though!

# 6

# Document Enhancements

In this section we discuss features that can enhance a document's appearance, such as page numbering, using headers and footers, or footnotes, how to create a document with multiple columns, how to incorporate text boxes, and how to import pictures into frames.

## Page Numbering

If you need to number the pages of a document you use the **Insert, Page Numbers** command, which displays the dialogue box shown in Fig. 6.1 below.

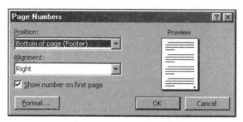

Fig. 6.1 The Page Numbers Dialogue Box

Fig. 6.2 Number Formats

You use this box to specify the position of the page numbers in your document and their alignment. You can also select whether to **Show number on first page** or not. Clicking the **Format** button, opens the Page Number Format dialogue box we show here in Fig. 6.2.

From this box you can select the **Number format** from the following alternatives, '1, - 1 -, a, A, i, or I'; the more usual style being the first option, as used in this book. The 'Page numbering' option gives you two alternatives; **Continue from previous section**, or **Start at** a specified number.

Some explanation is needed here. You can, with Word, split a document up into different sections, with each section having different page formats, headers and footers or page numbering. You do this by adding section breaks from the Break box shown earlier in Fig. 4.9 on page 76.

To illustrate page numbering, open the **PC Users4** document and use the **Insert, Page Numbers** command. Then, select 'Center' from the **Alignment** list box and make sure that the **Show number on First page** box is ticked. Next, press the **Format** button, select **Start at 1** at the bottom of the second dialogue box, and click the **OK** button on each dialogue box. The result is a number '1' appearing centrally in a footer at the bottom of page 1, as shown below.

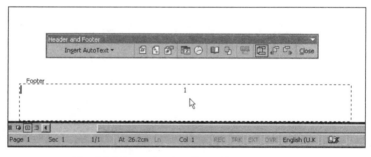

Fig. 6.3 A Page Number Placed in a Footer Box

If you double-click this 'greyed' page number the Footer area will be opened ready for editing, as shown in Fig. 6.3 above. This area is dotted and has description text above its top line, 'Footer' in our example above. The Header and Footer toolbar will also be displayed to help you control the content and editing of the footer.

Finally, save the current document as **PC Users5**.

# Using Headers and Footers

Headers consist of text placed in the top margin area of a page, whereas footers are text in the bottom margin. Simple headers or footers in Word can consist of text and a page number, which are produced in the same position of every page in a document, while more complicated ones can also contain graphics images.

Word allows you to have one header/footer for the first page of a document, or section of a document, and different ones for the rest of the document. It also allows you to select a different header or footer for odd or even pages.

To insert a header or footer in a document, select the **View, Header and Footer** command, which displays the following toolbar and Header insertion area.

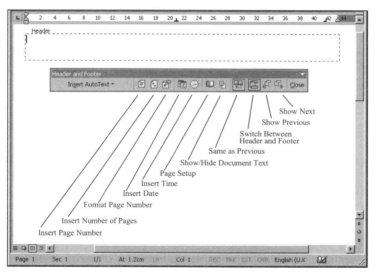

Fig. 6.4 The Header and Footer Toolbar Explained

From here, you can use the individual buttons to add your header information. For example, you can insert a page number and format it, insert the current date and time, or use the page set-up option to create a different header or footer for the first page of a document, or create different headers and footers for odd and even pages. You can also show and hide the document text, create similar headers and footers in a section to those of a previous section, or jump to the previous or next header and footer.

You can also click the **Insert AutoText** button to access one of the displayed options to automatically insert formatted information in your headers and footers, as shown in our composite example Fig. 6.5 below.

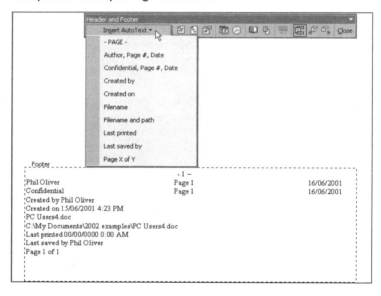

Fig. 6.5 The 10 Options in the AutoText Menu

This example shows the options available in the Insert AutoText sub-menu, with the results of each placed below.

Once you select the **Close** button, headers and footers can be formatted and edited like any other text. To edit a header or footer, simply point to the appropriate panel and double-click. The Header and Footer bar will appear on the screen and from then on you can use the editing and formatting commands, or the buttons available to you on the Formatting toolbar.

# Footnotes and Endnotes

If your document requires **footnotes** at the end of each page, or **endnotes** at the end of each chapter, they are very easy to add and later, if necessary, to edit. Place the cursor where you want the reference point to be in the document and select **Insert, Foot<u>n</u>ote**, which opens the following dialogue box.

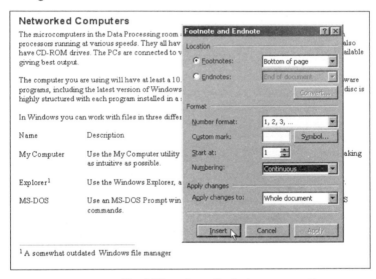

Fig. 6.6 Inserting a Footnote

This displays both the box and the results obtained, on the same screen. The reference point was placed after the word 'Explorer'. The text for the footnote is typed after pressing the **Insert** button.

The default option in the dialogue box is **Footnotes** at the **Bottom of page**. To place an endnote you would obviously select **Endnotes** instead. You can change the **Number format**, and set what number to **Start at**.

To use a reference mark of your own choosing, then type or paste it in the **Custom mark** box, or click the **Symbol** button and choose from the Symbol box shown in Fig. 5.20.

## Using Multiple Columns on a Page

You can quickly modify the number of displayed columns, for a selected part of a document or section by using the **Columns** button from the toolbar, shown here. However, if you want more control over how the columns are displayed, then use the **Format, Columns** command.

In Fig. 6.7 below, we have selected the first paragraph of the **PC Users5** memo and then used the **Format, Columns** command to format it into two columns with 3.6 ch in between the two columns, and a **Line between**.

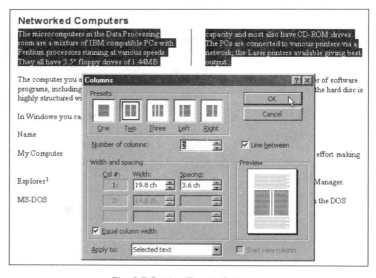

Fig. 6.7 Setting Text in Columns

To see how the 'Preview' page changes, click the appropriate button on the **Presets** field of this Columns dialogue box. Now change the **Spacing** (otherwise known as gutter width) to see how to set the separation zones between columns.

In the **Number of columns** box you can choose up to 12 columns. The **Apply to** option controls whether the columns are applied to the text selected, or the rest of the document.

# Text Boxes and Frames

Word 2002 uses both text boxes and frames, which can best be thought of as containers for text that can be positioned on a page and sized.

Before Word 97, only frames were available and were used whenever you wanted to wrap text around a graphic or framed text. Now you can wrap text around a graphic of any size or shape without first inserting it in a text box or frame. However, when opening a document created in earlier versions of Word which contains a graphic in a frame, Word opens it with a frame around it.

Text boxes, which were first used in Word 97, provide nearly all the advantages of frames, plus a lot more besides. For example, you can make text flow from one part of a document to another part by putting it in text boxes and linking them together. So for most cases with ordinary documents, a text box is preferable, but you must use a frame when you want to position text or graphics that contain comments, footnotes or end-notes, fields used for numbering lists and paragraphs in legal documents and outlines, tables of contents and index entries. They are also used extensively when developing certain types of Web pages.

It is perhaps worth while at this point spending some time with the Ask a Question box exploring the differences between frames and text boxes. To do so, type 'frames' into the text window, as shown in Fig. 6.8, and press the <Enter> key. This will then display a help menu as shown here.

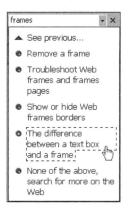

Fig. 6.8
Help on Frames

Selecting each item in turn, produces further useful help screens on the subject.

## The New Drawing Canvas

A new feature to Word 2002 is the drawing canvas which is placed around text boxes and drawing objects when they are inserted into a document. Anything placed onto a drawing canvas is 'separated' from the background document. When you move the canvas, everything on it moves together. When you re-size the canvas all the objects on it are re-scaled together.

The canvas helps you arrange the drawings and text boxes in the document. When first placed, a drawing canvas has no background or border, but you can control these and many other features in the Format Drawing Canvas dialogue box which opens when you double-click on the canvas.

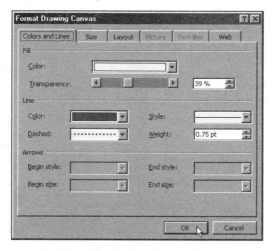

Fig. 6.9 Setting Drawing Canvas Features

## Inserting Text Boxes

With Word you can create an empty text box by using the **Insert, Text Box** command. If you are not in Page Layout mode, the program will automatically switch you to it on selection of this command. The program then opens a new drawing canvas and the cursor changes to a cross-hair, as shown in Fig. 6.10 on the next page.

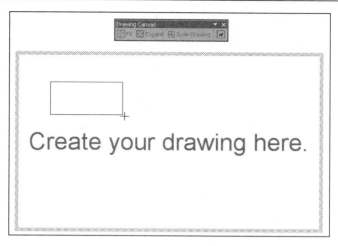

Fig. 6.10 Creating a Text Box

To create the text box, move the cross to the desired position and drag it to the shape you want. You can do this inside, or outside of the drawing canvas. If you place it outside, the canvas will disappear.

Releasing the left mouse button, fixes the text box in position in your document with the insertion point blinking in the upper left corner within the text box. When you type text, it wraps to fit the text box, but if you type more lines than can be accommodated within the text box, as in Fig. 6.11, you will have to increase its vertical size manually to see all the text.

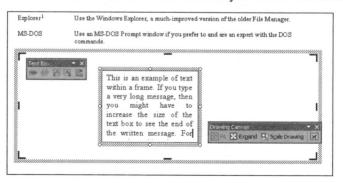

Fig. 6.11 Typing Text into a Text Box

## Moving Text Boxes

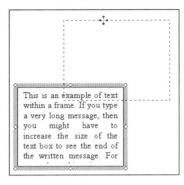

Fig. 6.12 Dragging a Text Box

A text box can be moved around your document by first selecting it, then dragging it with the mouse (move the mouse pointer over the edge of the text box until it turns to a four-headed arrow, as shown in Fig. 6.12, then click and drag to the desired position). The dotted outline shows the position in which the frame will be placed once you let go the mouse button.

Another way of moving a text box is by first selecting it, then using the **Format, Text Box** command to display the Format Text Box, which is shown in Fig. 6.13 below, with its Layout tab depressed.

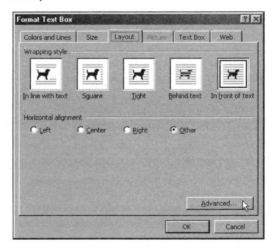

Fig. 6.13 The Format Text Box Dialogue Box

Next, click the **Advanced** button to display an additional dialogue box, shown next in Fig. 6.14.

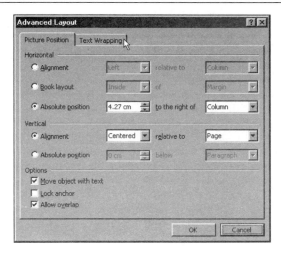

Fig. 6.14 Controlling the Layout of a Text Box

In this box you can specify the exact position of the text box. You also have the option of anchoring the box in that exact position, or allowing it to move with the document text.

Pressing the Text Wrapping tab of the Advanced Layout dialogue box above, opens the one shown in Fig. 6.15 below.

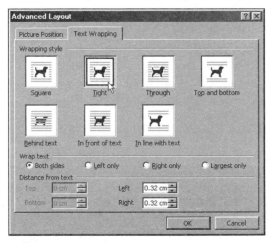

Fig. 6.15 The Advanced Layout Dialogue Box

This allows you to specify the wrapping options when a text box is placed in the middle of an existing paragraph. If you select a wrapping style other than **Top & bottom**, then format the text into two columns, as discussed on page 118, before inserting the text box - it will look much better.

Wrapping style options can be selected on the Text Wrapping tabbed sheet of the Advanced Layout dialogue box shown in Fig. 6.15 on the previous page. The default wrapping style is **In front of text**. To see what appears in our screen dump, click the **Tight** option, which also activates the **Wrap text** options in the dialogue box, with **Both sides** being the default.

Once the suggested selections have been made your document should look something like ours in Fig. 6.16 below.

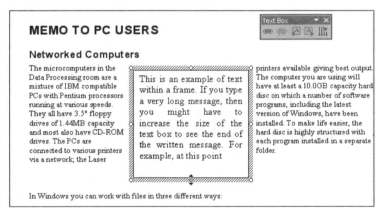

Fig. 6.16 The Text Box Placed in Position

The small Text Box toolbar at the top right-hand side of the above display allows you to create and break forward text box links, to go to the previous and next text box, change text direction and change the text direction in the box.

## Sizing Text Boxes

There are two ways of sizing text boxes; with the mouse, or with the keyboard using the Size tab on the Format Text Box.

*Sizing a Text Box with the Mouse*: To size a text box with the mouse, select it so that the round selection handles appear around the text box, then move the mouse pointer over one of the selection handles until it turns to the two-headed sizing arrow, as shown in Fig. 6.16. Drag the sizing arrow to change the text box to the required size, then release the mouse button.

Dragging one of the corner handles will drag the two attached text box sides with the pointer, but dragging a centre line handle will only move that side. Try these actions until you are happy with the resultant text box.

*Sizing a Text Box with the Keyboard:* To size a text box with the keyboard, first select it, then use the **Format, Text Box** command which displays the Format Text Box dialogue box, shown in Fig. 6.13. In this box, click the Size tab, then specify the **Height** and **Width** of the required text box.

## Rotating Text in a Text Box

Once you have your text box with its contents where you want it on the page, you can rotate it, using the **Change Text Direction** button on the Text Box bar, as shown in Fig. 6.17 below.

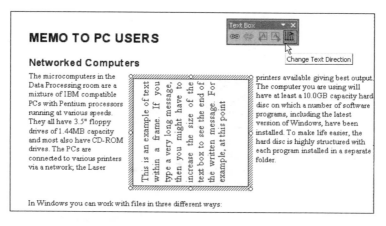

Fig. 6.17 Rotating the Text Direction in a Text Box

Next, click the mouse button outside the text box, which will cancel the text box selection; you will then not be able to access, or edit, the text inside it until you next click inside the text box. Finally, save this as **PC Users6**.

Moving the mouse pointer over the sides of the text box, turns it into a four-headed arrow, allowing you to move the text box to a new position when you click and drag. You can select the text box by single clicking which will let you re-size it, and if you clicked anywhere on the text within the text box, will also allow you to edit that text.

## Importing a Picture

Word 2002 has been given much more power in the finding, organising and displaying of graphic images such as photographs and clip art.

When you use the **Insert, Picture, Clip Art** command to import a graphic into a document, Word now opens the Insert Clip Art Task Pane shown in Fig. 6.18.

This pane works in conjunction with the new Clip Organizer, as we shall soon see. Before we look at that though, try placing the Media Content CD that came with Office XP into your CD drive and type the word 'koala' into the **Search text** box, as we show here. Then click the **Search** button.

Fig. 6.18 The Insert Clip Art Task Pane

With us this searched the CD for references to the search word and found just three relevant pictures, as shown in the Task Pane of Fig. 6.19 on the next page.

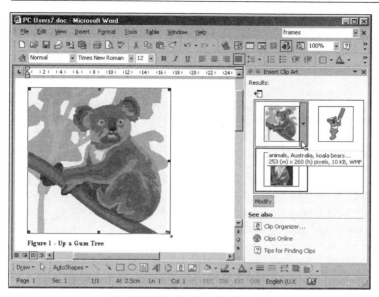

Fig. 6.19 Clip Art Search Results

Clicking any of these, placed it in the document at the insertion point position. Clicking the selection down-arrow on one (as shown above) opens a context menu of actions you can take. From this, the **Preview/Properties** command lets you preview the picture as shown in Fig. 6.20.

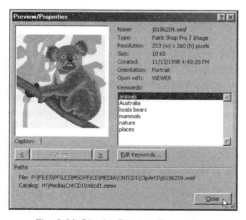

Fig. 6.20 Clip Art Preview/Properties

When you select the inserted image, by clicking it, a series of black squares is placed round it. Dragging any of these square handles lets you re-size the graphic, as we described earlier with text boxes.

As you should expect by now, pointing to a graphic and right-clicking it displays a shortcut menu, the **Format Picture** option of which opens the Format Picture dialogue box. This is almost the same as the Format Text Box dialogue, we covered earlier and shown in Fig. 6.13. This allows you to select the wrapping style, as discussed earlier. This is important, as by default an inserted picture is placed **In line with text** and unless you change this you will not be able to move it around your document. We suggest you play around with these settings until you are happy with them.

## The Picture Bar

Fig. 6.21 The
Picture Bar

If you want to change a picture you have inserted into your document, you can use the **View, Toolbars** command and select **Picture** from the drop-down menu. This opens the floating Picture Bar with a range of tools that can be used to manipulate pictures to suit your needs. Their functions are named in Fig. 6.21 on the left.

Try using these tools on the imported image to see how you can enhance or utterly destroy it! If, at the end of the day, you don't save it, it doesn't matter what you do to it. And if it came from the CD even that would be no problem! Just experiment.

# The Clip Organizer

As we saw on page 126 the Insert Clip Art Task Pane lets you search for photos, clip art and other media files on keywords and titles. The search can be restricted to any of your disc drives, folders or can include on-line sites on the Internet.

The Clip Organizer is a new facility to help you organise your media files into separate collections on your hard disc so that you can easily find them later. The first time you open the Clip Organizer, from the Insert Clip Art pane, you can choose to let it scan your computer for photos and other media files. It does not actually copy or move the files but creates shortcuts to them in collection folders.

Once it has done this an Explorer type window opens up like ours in Fig. 6.22 below.

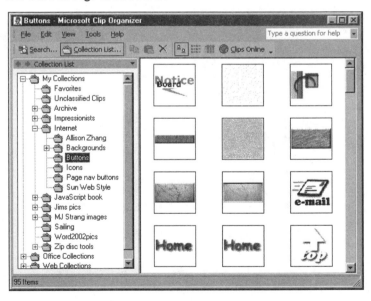

Fig. 6.22 The Clip Organizer Window

If all is well, every graphic image on your computer will be listed in different folders under the 'My Collections' entry in the Collection List, which uses the left pane of the window. The Clip Organizer places your images in sub-folders that reflect the name of the folder in which they were found on the scanned disc. As you select a folder in this list its contents are shown as thumbnail images in the right pane.

If for any reason this list gets corrupted, as it has once with us, there is an easy remedy. All the catalogue details are saved in the file mstore10.mgc. Find the file with the Windows **Start**, **Sea_rch**, **For _F_iles or Folders** facility, delete it and then reboot your computer. To re-catalogue your media, open the Clip Organizer and use the **_F_ile _A_dd Clips to Organizer**, **Auto_m_atically** commands.

## Organising Your Pictures

We saw in Fig. 6.20 that the artwork on the Media Content CD is well organised. Each picture has several keywords to help a search operation, and the files are grouped into a logical folder structure. On the CD you cannot change any of these, but the data on your hard disc(s) will almost certainly need organising. Keywords are added from the Preview/ Properties box we described on page 127.

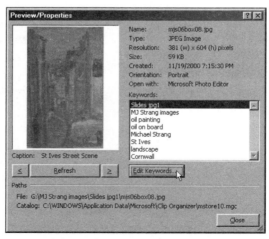

Fig. 6.23 Viewing a Picture and its Properties

Fig. 6.23 shows another example of this dialogue box, but one that can be edited as the file is on our hard disc. To do this click the **Edit Keywords** button to open the Keywords box shown in Fig. 6.24 below.

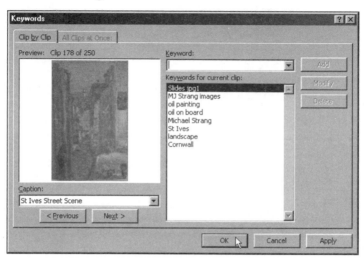

Fig. 6.24 Adding Keywords and Captions

In this box you can type a picture **Caption**, or name, and enter a new keyword, or edit an existing one. For more assistance, you can always click the **Help** button, the Organizer has its own Help System as shown in Fig. 6.25.

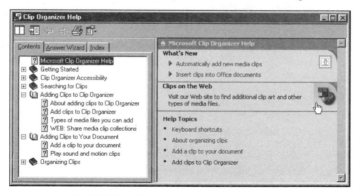

Fig. 6.25 The Organizer Help Opening Screen

# Inserting Picture Files

If you know where a picture file is that you want to insert into a document, there is a quicker way to place it there. You can use the **Insert**, **Picture**, **From File** command and select from the box shown below in Fig. 6.26.

Fig. 6.26 Inserting a Picture

By default, this box opens in the Windows My Pictures folder, but you can open any of your folders from the **Look in** drop-down list.

Fig. 6.27 Compressing Pictures

To format a photograph in your document, select it and use the **Format**, **Picture** command. The options are similar to those seen earlier, except for the new **Compress** button. This opens the box shown here, in which you can change the resolution of some or all the pictures in a file. For screen images, used for Web pages, a resolution of 96 dpi (dots per inch) produces a much smaller document file. If you are printing the document, leave the setting at **Print**, which saves images at 200 dpi.

# The Drawing Object Tools

In Word you can use the Drawing tools to create, or edit, a drawing consisting of graphic objects, such as lines, arcs, ellipses, rectangles, and other shapes. These can either exist in their own right, or be additions to a picture or object.

When you want to create a drawing in your document, use the **Insert**, **Picture**, **New Drawing** command which places a new drawing canvas in your document at the insertion point, as shown in Fig. 6.28 below.

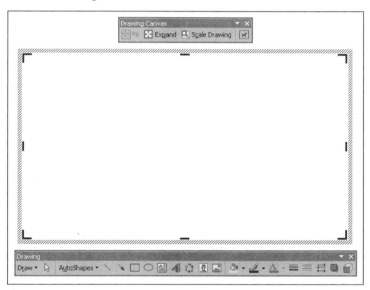

Fig. 6.28 A New Drawing Canvas with Toolbars

Two toolbars are opened as well, in our example, that to control the drawing canvas is shown above, and the Drawing toolbar which contains the actual drawing tools below. You can move these around the screen, or dock them onto one of the window sides.

The drawing canvas itself forms a 'container' to hold the drawing objects you place onto it. Once there they will move, or re-size, with the canvas, without you having to group them together, as with previous versions of Word.

# The Drawing Toolbar

Fig. 6.29 The
Drawing Toolbar

The various functions offered by the Drawing toolbar are shared by all Office XP applications and give Word a superior graphics capability. Amongst the many features available are:

**AutoShapes** – the AutoShape categories, such as connectors, block arrows, flowchart symbols, stars and banners, callouts, and action buttons make drawing diagrams much easier.

**Bezier curves** – used to easily create exact curves with pinpoint precision.

**3-D effects** – allow you to transform 2-D shapes into realistic 3-D objects with 3-D effects, such as changing the lighting perspective of a 3-D object.

**Perspective shadows** – allow you to select from a wide range of shadows with perspective, and you can adjust the depth and angle of each shadow to make pictures more realistic.

**Arrowhead styles** – allow you to change the width and height of arrowheads for maximum effect.

**Object alignment** – allows you to distribute and space objects evenly, both horizontally and vertically.

**Precise line-width control** – allows you increased control over the width of lines by selecting pre-set options or customised line widths.

**Transparent background** – background colours can be turned into transparent areas. These can now be graded with slider controls to give very professional results.

## Creating a Drawing

To create an object, click on the required Drawing button, such as the <u>O</u>val or <u>R</u>ectangle, position the mouse pointer where you want to create the object on the drawing canvas, and then drag the mouse to draw the object. Hold the <Shift> key while you drag the mouse to create a perfect circle or square. If you do not hold <Shift>, Word creates an oval or a rectangle.

You can use the **AutoShapes** button to select from a variety of pre-drawn **Lines**, **Basic Shapes**, etc. First open the menu bars and click on the desired line or shape, then position the mouse pointer where you want to create the object on the canvas and click the left mouse button to place it.

Fig. 6.30
Autoshape Options

All of the Autoshape graphical sub-menus can be dragged off the menu and floated on the screen for easy access. Fig. 6.31 is a composite showing all the standard Autoshape options.

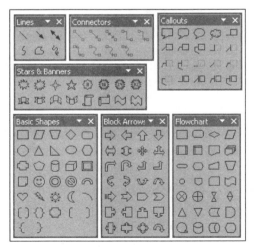

Fig. 6.31 The Seven 'Floating' Autoshape Menus

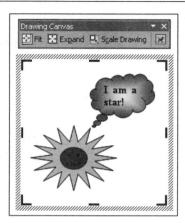

Fig. 6.32 Some Objects Placed on the Drawing Canvas

## Editing a Drawing

To select an object, click on it. Word displays white handles around the object selected. Shapes can be re-sized, rotated, flipped, coloured, and combined to make more complex shapes. Some AutoShapes have a coloured adjustment handle that you can use to change the most prominent feature of a shape — for example, the star above has variable depth rays.

You can move an object, or multiple objects, within the canvas by selecting them and dragging to the desired position. To copy an object, click it, then use the **Edit, Copy** / **Edit, Paste** commands or toolbar buttons.

To size an object, position the mouse pointer on a white handle and then drag the handle until the object is the desired shape and size.

To delete an object, select it and press the <Del> key. To delete a drawing, just delete the canvas.

## Placing a Drawing

Once you are happy with your drawing you can use the Drawing Canvas toolbar, shown on Fig. 6.32, to place it at the correct location in your document.

Fig. 6.33
Wrapping Options

Clicking the **Fit** button will shrink the canvas to the size of the drawing. The **Expand** button enlarges the canvas a little, every time it is clicked. Neither of these buttons affect the drawing itself. The **Scale Drawing** button places hollow white handles around the canvas. You drag these in the normal Windows way to enlarge, or shrink, both the canvas and all of the objects on it. This is a very powerful feature.

Before you can move the canvas you will need to click the **Text Wrapping** button shown here in Fig. 6.33 with its menu options. By default a canvas is placed **In Line With Text** and will only move when the text around it moves.

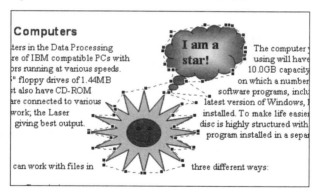

Fig. 6.34 Editing Drawing Canvas Wrapping Points

In Fig. 6.34 we selected **Tight** wrapping and dragged the canvas to where we wanted it. As can be seen, the surrounding text wraps tightly over the canvas. You can even control how this happens by selecting **Edit Wrap Points**, as shown above, and dragging any of the square points. Do try out some of these effects, they really are fun.

# Diagrams and Organisation Charts

Another new feature of Word 2002 is the ability to easily create highly customised diagrams and organisation type charts. You do this by clicking the **Insert Diagram or Organisation Charts** button on the Drawing toolbar, shown here, and using the diagramming tools that are then available in the Diagram Gallery.

Fig. 6.35 The Diagram Gallery

## Diagram Types

Six types of diagrams are available for you to work with, which would usually be used in the following ways.

**Organisation Chart** - Used for hierarchical relationships, such as the management structure of a company.

**Cycle** - Used to show a process that has a continuous cycle.

**Target** - Used to show steps toward a goal.

**Radial** - Used to show relationships of elements to a core element.

**Venn** - Used to show areas of overlap between and among elements.

**Pyramid** - Used to show foundation-based relationships.

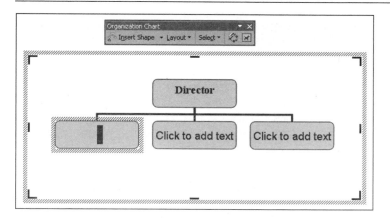

Fig. 6.36 Starting an Organization Chart

In Fig. 6.36 above we show how an organization chart can be started. The above text boxes were automatically added to the drawing canvas shown. You enter the text you want and format it. You add extra shape boxes and control the layout and style of the chart from the Organization Chart toolbar options.

We do not have the space here to delve any deeper into this facility. There would almost be the scope for another book! It is well worth getting to grips, though, and using diagrams to illustrate your material and enliven your documents. Don't forget the Help system if you want more detail. It covers this feature quite well, unlike some of the others.

# Inserting Objects into a Document

You can insert 'Objects' into a Microsoft Word document to include information created in other Office programs or in many other Windows programs. An Object can take the form of a table, chart, graphic, equation, or other type of information. (In case you wondered, Objects created in one application, for example spreadsheets, and linked or embedded in another application are called OLE Objects.)

To insert an Object into a document you use the **Insert, Object** command which opens the dialogue box shown in Fig. 6.37 below. From this, you can choose different 'Object types', from say a Lotus 1-2-3 Worksheet or a WordPad Document.

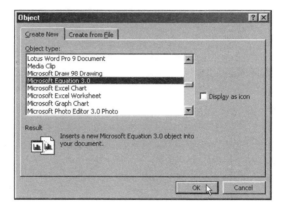

Fig. 6.37 The Object Dialogue Box

Word may take several seconds to open this box as it scans your system to build the list of Object types you can use, depending on the software that you have installed.

For example, if you select 'Microsoft Equation 3.0' from the **Object type** list, as shown above, Word displays the Equation Editor which allows you to build mathematical equations in your Word document. This should have been installed with Office XP and is, in fact, the same editor that was included in earlier versions of Microsoft Office.

## Inserting an Equation

If building equations is not your cup of tea, you can safely skip this section. If, on the other hand, you want to learn how to build equations, activate the Equation Editor from the above box.

Fig. 6.38 The Microsoft Equation Editor

This places an equation box at the insertion point and opens the Equation toolbar, as shown in Fig. 6.38. We suggest you first press **F1** to display the Help screen shown in Fig. 6.39.

Fig. 6.39 The Equation Editor Help System

Selecting the first option, reveals a further list of topics under it, as shown. Working through these will give a good introduction and tell you about the Equation toolbar and how you can use it. It is an 'older' Help system though and is not quite as easy to get around as the main Word help.

The top row of the Equation Editor toolbar has buttons for inserting more than 150 mathematical symbols, many of which are not available in the Symbol dialogue box described on page 111.

To insert a symbol in an equation, click a button on the top row of the toolbar, as shown on the composite screen dump below, and then click the specific symbol from the palette that appears under the button.

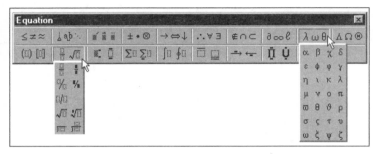

Fig. 6.40 Using the Equation Editor

The bottom row of the Equation Editor toolbar has buttons for inserting templates or frameworks that contain such symbols as fractions, radicals, summations, integrals, products, matrices, and various fences or matching pairs of symbols such as brackets and braces. There are about 120 templates, grouped on palettes, many of which contain slots - spaces into which you type text and insert symbols. Templates can be nested, by inserting them in the slots of other templates, to build complex hierarchical formulae.

Finally, select the second recommended help topic to find out about spacing and alignment, expanding templates, styles, embellishments, and how to position the insertion pointer so that you can achieve best results.

As an example, we will take you through the steps required, when using the Equation Editor, to construct the equation for the solution of a quadratic equation, as shown here.

$$x = \frac{-b \pm \sqrt{\{b^2 - 4ac\}}}{2a}$$

To construct this equation, place the insertion pointer at the required place in your document, activate the Equation Editor, and follow the steps listed below. The templates and symbols you require from the Equation Editor are shown to the right of the appropriate step.

- Type **x =** followed by selecting the template shown here from the lower second button.

- Type **–b** followed by selecting the ± symbol from the upper fourth button.

- Select the square root template shown here from the lower second button.

- Select the brackets template shown here from the lower first button.

- Type **b** followed by selecting the template from the lower third button.

- Type **2** and re-position the insertion pointer as shown here, and then type **–4ac**.

- Position the insertion pointer at the denominator and type **2a**.

Obviously, the Equation Editor is capable of a lot more than we have covered here, but this simple example should serve to get you started. Try it, it's simpler than it looks.

# 7

# Using Tables and Graphs

The ability to use 'Tables' is built into most top-range word processors these days. At first glance the process might look complicated and perhaps only a small percentage of users take advantage of the facility, which is a pity because using a Table has many possibilities. If you have worked with a spreadsheet, such as Excel or Lotus 1-2-3, then you are familiar with the principle of tables.

Tables are used to create adjacent columns of text and numeric data. A table is simply a grid of columns and rows with the intersection of a column and row forming a rectangular box which is referred to as a 'cell'. In Word you can include pictures, charts, notes, footnotes, tabs, other tables and page breaks in your tables. There are several ways to place information into a table:

- Type the desired text, or numeric data.

- Paste text from the main document.

- Link two tables within a document.

- Insert data created in another application.

- Import a picture.

- Create a chart on information held in a table.

The data is placed into individual cells that are organised into columns and rows, similar to a spreadsheet. You can modify the appearance of table data by applying text formatting and enhancements, or by using different styles.

# Creating a Table

 Tables can be created either by clicking the **Insert Table** button on the toolbar, shown here, or by using the **Table, Insert, Table** command. Using the latter method, displays the dialogue box shown in Fig. 7.1, which lets you size the column widths at that point.

Fig. 7.1 Inserting a Table

As an example we will step through the process of creating the table shown in Fig. 7.3 on page 148. Open a 'New' file (it could be an existing file, in which case you place the insertion point where you want the table to appear), then click on the **Insert Table** button and drag down and to the right.

As you drag the mouse, the **Insert Table** button expands to create a grid of rows and columns, as shown in Fig. 7.2. At the bottom of the box there is an automatic display of the number of rows and columns you are currently selecting. When you release the mouse button, a table is inserted in your document the size of the selected grid.

Fig. 7.2 Using
The Table Button

For our example, we require a 10 x 5 table with 10 rows and 5 columns of cells. Once this appears in position in the document, the cursor is placed in the top left cell awaiting your input. The cells forming the table, are displayed with lines around each cell. To move around in a table, simply click the desired cell to select it, or use one of the keyboard commands listed on the next page.

## Navigating with the Keyboard

To navigate around a table when using the keyboard, use the following keys:

| *Press this* | *To do this* |
|---|---|
| Tab | Moves the insertion point right one cell, in the same row, and from the last cell in one row to the first cell in the next row. If the cell contains information it highlights the contents. |
| Shift+Tab | Moves the insertion point left one cell. If the cell contains information it highlights the contents. |
| $\uparrow, \downarrow, \leftarrow$, and $\rightarrow$ | Moves the insertion point within cells, between cells, and between the cells in a table and the main document text. |
| Home | Moves the insertion point to the beginning of the current line within a cell. |
| Alt+Home | Moves the insertion point to the first column in the current row. |
| End | Moves the insertion point to the end of the current line within a cell. |
| Alt+End | Moves the insertion point to the last column in the current row. |
| Alt+PgUp | Moves the insertion point to the top cell in the column. |
| Alt+PgDn | Moves the insertion point to the bottom cell in the column. |

Now type in the information given below and format your table using the buttons on the Formatting toolbar to align the contents of the various cells as shown.

| Types of Removable Discs | | | | |
|---|---|---|---|---|
| Description | Capacity Kbytes | Price/Unit Pence | Number Bought | Cost in £ |
| | | | | |
| Double-density diskettes | 720 | 30 | 60 | |
| High-density diskettes | 1,440 | 40 | 80 | |
| Removable Zip discs | 100,000 | 500 | 6 | |
| Removable Zip discs | 250,000 | 1,300 | 4 | |
| Removable hard discs | 1,500,000 | 5,800 | 1 | |
| | | | | ———— |
| | | | Total | |

Fig. 7.3 Our Example Table

To enter the heading as shown, highlight all the cells of the first row, then use the **Table, Merge Cells** command to join all the cells into one. Now you can type the heading, centre it, format it in bold, and increase its font size to your liking.

The line in the cell of the penultimate row and last column was entered using the **Insert, Symbol** command, and selecting a line character (code 190) from the Symbol font. Inserting this character repeatedly, gives a continuous horizontal line. A much easier way, though, would be to use the Tables and Borders floating toolbar, as shown here in Fig. 7.4.

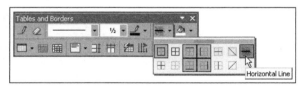

Fig. 7.4 The Tables and Borders Toolbar

With all the Table commands in one set of buttons, this toolbar makes most operations very much easier. As with all toolbars in Word, it is opened from the **View, Toolbars** main menu command.

# Changing Column Width and Row Height

The column width of selected cells or entire columns can be changed by dragging the table column markers on the ruler or by dragging the column boundaries, as shown in Fig. 7.5.

Fig. 7.5 Changing Column Width

You can also drag a column boundary while holding down certain keys. The overall effects of these actions being:

| *Key used* | *Effect* |
|---|---|
| No key | Only the columns to the left and right are re-sized proportionally with the overall width of the table remaining the same size. |
| Shift key | Only the column to the left is re-sized with the overall width of the table changing by the same amount. |
| Ctrl key | As the column to the left changes, all columns to the right change proportionally, but the overall width of the table remains the same. |

The height of a row depends on its contents. As you type text into a cell, its height increases to accommodate it. You can increase the height of a cell by inserting empty lines before or after the text by pressing the <Enter> key. All other cells in that row become the same height as the largest cell. You can also increase the height of rows by dragging a row boundary up or down, as shown in Fig. 7.6.

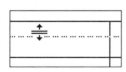

Fig. 7.6 Changing
Row Height

The width of a column and the height of a row can also be changed by using the **Table, Table Properties** command to display a dialogue box with appropriate tabs for controlling size and the placement of a table, the column and row size, as well as the alignment of entries within cells.

When you have finished, save your work so far under the filename **Table 1**. We will use this table to show you how you can insert expressions into cells to make your table behave just like a spreadsheet.

## Entering Expressions

To enter an expression into a table cell, so that you can carry out spreadsheet type calculations, select the cell and use the **Table, Formula** command which displays the dialogue box shown on the next page. Word automatically analyses the table and suggests an appropriate formula in the **Formula** box of the displayed dialogue box, as shown in Fig. 7.7.

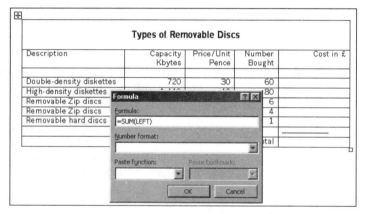

Fig. 7.7 Entering a Formula into a Cell

In the above situation, it has found numbers in cells to the left of the highlighted cell, therefore it suggests the SUM(LEFT) formula. To replace this formula, simply delete it from the **Formula** box and type the new formula preceded by the equal (=) sign.

For example, to calculate the cost of purchased discs in Sterling (£) in cell E4, type the following formula in the **Formula** box:

```
=C4*D4/100
```

Word performs mathematical calculations on numbers in cells and inserts the result of the calculation as a field in the cell that contains the insertion pointer. Cells are referred to as A1, A2, B1, B2, and so on, with the letter representing a column and the number representing a row. Thus, B3 refers to the hatched cell.

|   | A | B | C |
|---|---|---|---|
| 1 |   |   |   |
| 2 |   |   |   |
| 3 |   | ☐ |   |

When you use the **Table, Formula** command, Word assumes addition, unless you indicate otherwise, and proposes a sum based on the following rules:

- If the cell that contains the insertion pointer is at the intersection of a row and column and both contain numbers, Word sums the column. To sum the row, type =SUM(LEFT) or =SUM(RIGHT) in the **Formula** box, depending on the location of the insertion pointer.

- If the cell that contains the insertion pointer contains text or numbers, they are ignored.

- Word evaluates numbers beginning with the cell closest to the cell that contains the insertion pointer and continues until it reaches either a blank cell or a cell that contains text.

- If the numbers you are calculating include a number format, such as a £ sign, the result will also contain that format.

Fill in the rest of column E (unfortunately you will have to retype the formula in each cell as there is no apparent method of replication), then to calculate the total cost, place the insertion pointer in cell E9 and use the **Table, Formula** command. Word analyses your table and suggests the following function:

```
=SUM(ABOVE)
```

which is the correct formula in this case. When you press **OK**, Word calculates the result and places it in cell E9, as shown on the following page. Save your work again for future use, but this time with the filename **Table 2**.

| Types of Removable Discs | | | | |
|---|---|---|---|---|
| Description | Capacity Kbytes | Price/Unit Pence | Number Bought | Cost in £ |
| Double-density diskettes | 720 | 30 | 60 | 18 |
| High-density diskettes | 1,440 | 40 | 80 | 32 |
| Removable Zip discs | 100,000 | 500 | 6 | 30 |
| Removable Zip discs | 250,000 | 1,300 | 4 | 52 |
| Removable hard discs | 1,500,000 | 5,800 | 1 | 58 |
| | | | | |
| | | | Total | 190 |

Fig. 7.8 Example Table with Calculated Cells

As the result of a calculation is inserted as a field in the cell that contains the insertion pointer, if you change the contents of the referenced cells, you must update the calculation. To do this, select the field (the cell that contains the formula) by highlighting it and press the **F9** function key.

In a formula you can specify any combination of mathematical and logical operators from the following list.

| | |
|---|---|
| Addition | + |
| Subtraction | − |
| Multiplication | * |
| Division | / |
| Percent | % |
| Powers and roots | ^ |
| Equal to | = |
| Less than | < |
| Less than or equal to | <= |
| Greater than | > |
| Greater than or equal to | >= |
| Not equal to | < > |

The functions below accept references to table cells:

| | | |
|---|---|---|
| ABS( ) | AND( ) | AVERAGE( ) |
| COUNT( ) | DEFINED( ) | FALSE( ) |
| IF( ) | INT( ) | MAX( ) |
| MIN( ) | MOD( ) | NOT( ) |
| OR( ) | PRODUCT( ) | ROUND( ) |
| SIGN( ) | SUM( ) | TRUE( ) |

The main reason for using formulae in a table, instead of just typing in the numbers, is that formulae will still give the correct final answer even if some of the data is changed.

If you change any cells referenced in a calculation, you can update the calculation by selecting the field and then pressing **F9**. As Word table calculations have to be manually recalculated like this, it is usually better to use Microsoft Excel to perform complex calculations.

## Editing a Table

You can edit a table by inserting or deleting columns or rows, or by merging or splitting cells, as follows:

*To insert a column or row:* Select the cell where you want

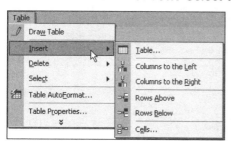

the new row or column to appear, then use the **Table**, **Insert** command and choose an option from the drop-down menu shown here in Fig. 7.9. This version of Word, allows you to insert columns or rows to either side of

Fig. 7.9 The Table Insert Sub-menu

the selected cell, as well as single cells.

*To delete a cell, a column or row:* Select the cell whose

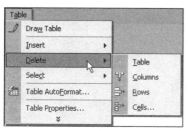

column or row you want to delete, then use the **Table, Delete** command and choose an option from the drop-down menu shown in Fig. 7.10. As you can see from the available options, you can even delete a single cell or an entire table.

Fig. 7.10 The Table Delete Sub-menu

*To merge cells:* Select the cells you want to merge, then use the **Table, Merge Cells** command.

*To split cells:* Move the insertion pointer to the cell you want to split, then use the **Table, Split Cells** command. The dialogue box shown in Fig. 7.11 is displayed which can be used to subdivide a cell.

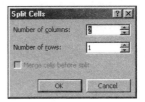

Fig. 7.11 Splitting Cells

*To split a table:* To split a table, click the row that you want to be the first row of the second table and select the **Table, Split Table** command. Using this command on the first row of a table, allows you to insert text before a table. In the example below (Fig. 7.12), the insertion pointer was placed in the second row before the table was split.

| Types of Removable Discs | | | | |
|---|---|---|---|---|
| Description | Capacity Kbytes | Price/Unit Pence | Number Bought | Cost in £ |
| Double-density diskettes | 720 | 30 | 60 | 18 |
| High-density diskettes | 1,440 | 40 | 80 | 32 |
| Removable Zip discs | 100,000 | 500 | 6 | 30 |
| Removable Zip discs | 250,000 | 1,300 | 4 | 52 |
| Removable hard discs | 1,500,000 | 5,800 | 1 | 58 |
| | | | | |
| | | | Total | 190 |

Fig. 7.12 Splitting a Table into Two

If you want to learn more about tables, place the insertion pointer inside a table, and type 'working with tables' into the Ask a Question box at the top of the Word window. Select the first item on the returned list, which with us was entitled 'About tables'. This option opens the Microsoft Word Help screen, which contains a wealth of information, the first part of which is shown in Fig. 7.13 on the next page.

**About tables**

A table is made up of rows and columns of cells that you can fill with text and graphics. Tables are often used to organize and present information.

You can also use tables to create interesting page layouts, or to create text, graphics and nested tables (nested table: A table inserted within a table cell. If you use a table to lay out a page, and you want to use another table to arrange the information, you can insert a nested table.) on a Web page.

▼ Parts of a table

Fig. 7.13 Microsoft Word's Help on Tables

# Formatting a Table

You can enhance the looks of a table by selecting one of many pre-defined styles. As an example, open the previously saved version of **Table 2**, place the insertion pointer in a table cell and use the **Table, Table AutoFormat** command. The following dialogue box appears on your screen.

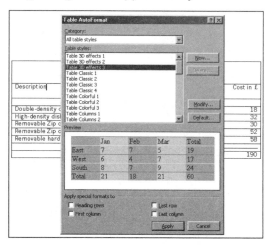

Fig. 7.14 Table AutoFormat Styles

We selected 'Table 3D effects' from the **Table styles** list, as shown in Fig. 7.14, to produce the following very professional looking table.

| Types of Removable Discs | | | | |
|---|---|---|---|---|
| Description | Capacity Kbytes | Price/Unit Pence | Number Bought | Cost in £ |
| Double-density diskettes | 720 | 30 | 60 | 18 |
| High-density diskettes | 1,440 | 40 | 80 | 32 |
| Removable Zip discs | 100,000 | 500 | 6 | 30 |
| Removable Zip discs | 250,000 | 1,300 | 4 | 52 |
| Removable hard discs | 1,500,000 | 5,800 | 1 | 58 |
| | | | Total | 190 |

Fig. 7.15 Our Table with Automatic Formatting Added

Finally, save the result of this formatting as **Table 3**.

# Using Microsoft Graph

To chart your Word data, you can use Microsoft Graph Chart, which can be activated with the **Insert, Object** command and selecting 'Microsoft Graph Chart' from the list in the Object dialogue box, shown below in Fig. 7.16.

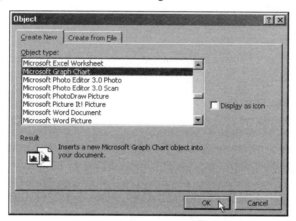

Fig. 7.16 Selecting a Graph Object

Pressing the **OK** button displays the following screen, provided no table was selected in your document.

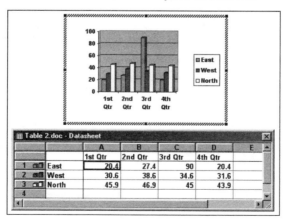

Fig. 7.17 The Word Default Graph and Datasheet

This is an internal Word example, showing the capabilities of the package. To demonstrate the way in which you can chart your own data in a Word table, open **Table 2** and then use your editing skills to transform it to what is displayed below.

| Removable Discs | Price/Unit Pence | Number Bought | Cost in £ |
|---|---|---|---|
| Double-density diskettes | 30 | 60 | 18 |
| High-density diskettes | 40 | 80 | 32 |
| Removable Zip discs | 150 | 6 | 30 |
| Removable Zip discs | 1300 | 4 | 52 |

Fig. 7.18 Data Prepared for Graphing

Note that we have replaced 'Description' with 'Removable Discs', and deleted the column dealing with 'Capacity Kbytes' and the row dealing with the removable hard discs (for the same charting limitations), as well as the empty row below the column headings.

Save the resultant work as **Table 4**. Then select the table, by either using the **Table, Select, Table** command, or highlighting it as shown in Fig. 7.19 below.

| Removable Discs | Price/Unit Pence | Number Bought | Cost in £ |
|---|---|---|---|
| Double-density diskettes | 30 | 60 | 18 |
| High-density diskettes | 40 | 80 | 32 |
| Removable Zip discs | 500 | 6 | 30 |
| Removable Zip discs | 1,300 | 4 | 52 |

Fig. 7.19 Data Selected For Graphing

Next, and while the table is selected, activate Microsoft Graph Chart by using the **Insert, Object** command and selecting 'Microsoft Graph Chart' from the list in the displayed Object dialogue box (see Fig. 7.16). Microsoft Graph Chart displays the table and chart shown in Fig. 7.20 on the next page.

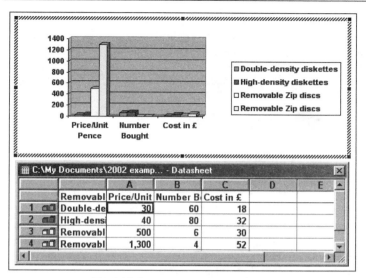

Fig. 7.20 Graph with Datasheet Below

When you click outside the graph area, the chart is embedded in your Word document. To move it, as with all of Word's graphics, select the graph, use the **Format**, **Object** menu command and on the Layout tabbed sheet change the **Wrapping style** from the default setting of **In line with text**. Once this is done you can simply drag the graph wherever you want in your document.

To edit a chart, double-click the chart area to display the Datasheet as shown in Fig. 7.20. When the Datasheet is activated, the menu bar option **Table** is replaced by two other menu options, **Data** and **Chart**. The respective sub-menus for these two are shown in Fig. 7.21 below.

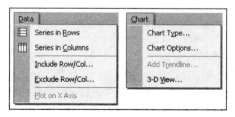

Fig. 7.21 The Data and Chart Menus

To display the captions in the first column of your table as the x-axis labels and those of the first row as the legends, use the **Data, Series by Columns** command. This displays the following screen:

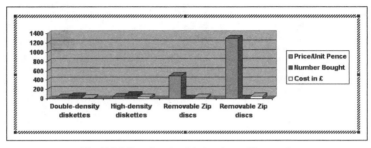

Fig. 7.22 Our Graph with the Axes Changed

# Pre-defined Chart Types

To select a different type of chart, use the **Chart, Chart Type** command which opens the box shown in Fig. 7.23 below.

Fig. 7.23 The Chart Type Dialogue Box

The Chart Type dialogue box lists 14 different chart options. These chart-types are normally used to describe the following relationships between data:

 **Area:** for showing a volume relationship between two series, such as production or sales, over a given length of time.

 **Bar:** for comparing differences in non-continuous data that are not related over time, by depicting changes in horizontal bars to show positive and negative variations from a given position.

 **Bubble:** for showing a type of XY (scatter) chart. The size of the data (radius of the bubble) indicates the value of a third variable.

 **Column:** for comparing separate items (non-continuous data which are related over time) by depicting changes in vertical bars to show positive and negative variations from a given position.

 **Cone:** for showing 3-D column and bar charts in a more dramatic way.

 **Cylinder:** similar to Cone.

 **Doughnut:** for comparing parts with the whole. Similar to pie charts, but can depict more than one series of data.

 **Line:** for showing continuous changes in data with time.

 **Pie:** for comparing parts with the whole. You can use this type of chart when you want to compare the percentage of an item from a single series of data with the whole series.

 **Pyramid:**    similar to Cone.

 **Radar:**    for plotting one series of data as angle values defined in radians, against one or more series defined in terms of a radius.

 **Surface:**    for showing optimum combinations between two sets of data, as in a topographic map. Colours and patterns indicate areas that are in the same range of values.

 **Stock:**    for showing high-low-close type of data variation to illustrate stock market prices or temperature changes.

 **XY (Scatter):**    for showing scatter relationships between X and Y. Scatter charts are used to depict items which are not related over time.

You can change the type of chart by selecting one of the fourteen alternate chart types from the Chart Type dialogue box, provided your data fits the selection. To preview your choice, select one **Chart sub-type** and press the **Press and Hold to View Sample** button on the dialogue box.

Clicking the Custom Types tab of the Chart Type dialogue box, reveals additional choices within the 14 main types of charts. For example, you can choose between several types of charts either in colour or in black and white, charts with logarithmic scale, or charts depicted as stacks of colours or even tubes.

## Improving a Microsoft Chart

A Microsoft Chart can be improved by using the Microsoft Draw facility (to activate it use the **View, Toolbars** command and click Drawing). We have used the **Arrow** and **Text Box** buttons on the Drawing toolbar to point to and annotate the 'Best Buy' on the chart shown below, and give it a title. As each value in the data used to create the chart is a separate object, it can be moved, changed, or formatted.

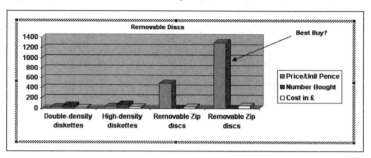

Fig. 7.24 Our Chart with some Customised Features Added

For example, clicking the chart title to select it, then using the **Format, Text Box** command, displays the dialogue box shown in Fig. 7.25 below.

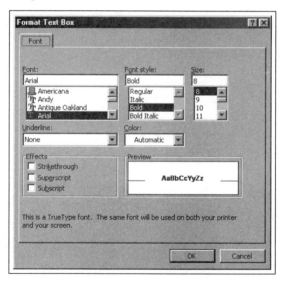

Fig. 7.25 The Format Text Box Dialogue Box

From here, you can change the Font, Alignment, Colours and Lines, Size, Properties, and Margins of the selected text box.

To further demonstrate some of the formatting capabilities of Microsoft Chart, you could use the Drawing facility to add a title to the 'Best Buy' data, then using the **Format, Text Box** command change the Font colour to white, click the Alignment tab and select a vertical orientation. The possibilities are endless.

When you have carried out all the required changes to your chart, save the Word document as **Table 5**.

We are sure that you will get many hours of fun with the various features of Microsoft Graph and, more to the point, produce some very professional graphics for your reports.

# 8

# Managing Your Documents

Many users' needs might demand that they work with either large documents, or with documents which are split into many files. In such cases, knowing something about outlines, file management and how to scan in documents from paper, will obviously be of use.

## Outline Mode

Outline mode provides a way of viewing and organising the contents of a document. Ten outline levels can be used and these can automatically be based on the default Word styles, (if they are used in your document), or on 'Levels' that you set yourself (Level 1 through to Level 9, plus Body text).

The following display shows part of the first page of Chapter 1 of this book in the normal Print Layout view.

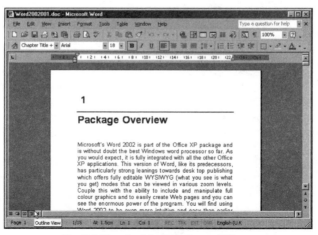

Fig. 8.1 Chapter 1 in Page Layout View

The same chapter is shown, in Fig. 8.2 below, in outline view obtained by either pressing the **Outline View** button on the horizontal scroll bar, or by selecting the **View, Outline** command. In our case we have not used the default Word styles for the document so before seeing exactly what is shown here, we had to assign Outline Levels to the various Headings. This is easily done by selecting the outline view and assigning levels to your work using the Outline Level tool on the outline bar which replaces the ruler.

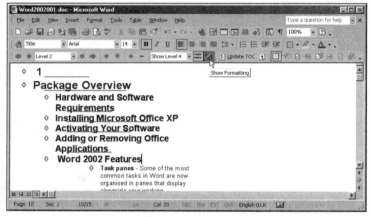

Fig. 8.2 Chapter 1 in Outline View

The actual formatting can only be seen if the **Show Formatting** button (the one pointed to above) is clicked.

## The Outlining Toolbar

This toolbar opens automatically when you change to outline view mode. It has been redesigned for version 2002 of Word and also contains buttons to control the Master Documents feature covered later. The functions of the buttons are:

***Button***          ***Function***

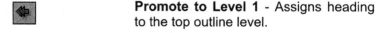          **Promote to Level 1** - Assigns heading to the top outline level.

**Promote** - Assigns heading to the next higher outline level.

 **Outline Level** - The list of available levels. This is used to manually set outline levels to your document paragraphs.

 **Demote** - Assigns to the next lower outline level.

 **Demote to Body Text** - Assigns the active paragraph as body text.

 **Move Up** - Moves selected text before the paragraph preceding it.

 **Move Down** - Moves selected text after the paragraph following it.

 **Expand** - Displays hidden subordinate headings until text is reached.

 **Collapse** - Hides displayed subordinate text or lower level headings.

 **Show Level** - Displays all headings and text to the lowest selected level.

 **Show First Line Only** - Toggles between the display of all body text, or just the first line.

 **Show Formatting** - Shows or hides character formatting.

 **Update TOC** - Lets you update an existing table of Contents.

**Go to TOC** - Displays an existing table of Contents.

Using the expand and collapse commands, you can display the entire document or only selected text. Editing a document in Outline mode is simple because you can control the level of detail that displays and quickly see the structure of the document. If you want to focus on the main topics in the document, you can collapse the text to display only paragraph styles set to high outline levels. If you want to view additional detail, you can expand the text to display text using paragraph styles set to lower outline levels.

In case you were wondering, the other buttons on the Outline toolbar perform the following functions:

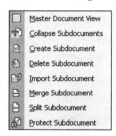

Fig. 8.3 The Other Buttons on the Outlining Toolbar

## Outline Symbols

Another feature of the outline view mode are the symbols placed before each paragraph (✿, ▭, and ▫). These not only show the status of the paragraph, but can be used to quickly manipulate paragraph text. Fig. 8.4 is from the Word Help System and graphically shows their meaning.

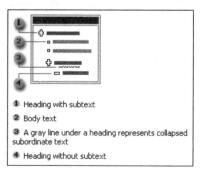

Fig. 8.4 The Symbols used in Outline View

To display, or hide, subordinate text double-click a ✛ button. Click on a ✛ button and drag it, to move text to a new location. Word automatically moves the text as you drag the mouse. When you drag a heading's symbol like this, the subheadings and body text under it also move or change levels. As you drag, Word displays a vertical line at each heading level. Release the mouse button to assign the text to that level. The corresponding heading level is applied to the heading, or Normal style is applied in the case of body text.

If you print from Outline View mode only the level of text that is seen on the screen will actually print. Remember that any embedded page breaks will be actioned in the print process, which can give some unusual results.

## Outline Numbering

If you want all your paragraphs numbered, you must rank all the styles, highlight all the paragraphs you want to number, and then assign one of the numbering schemes in the dialogue box obtained with the **Format, Bullets and**

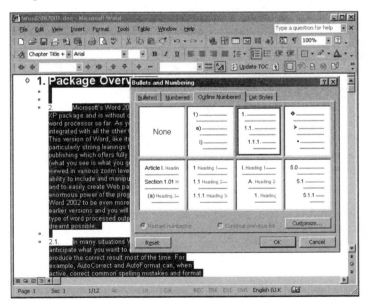

Fig. 8.5 Changing an Outline Numbering System

**Numbering** command. Click the **Numbered** tab, or if you want to modify the numbering system click the **Outline Numbered** tab, and choose from the dialogue box shown in Fig. 8.5 on the previous page.

# Creating a Table of Contents

To create a table of contents, undo the Numbered option, return to Page Layout and position the insertion point where you want the table of contents to appear. Next, use the **Insert**, **Reference**, **Index and Tables** command, and click the **Table of Contents** tab to display the dialogue box shown in Fig. 8.6 below.

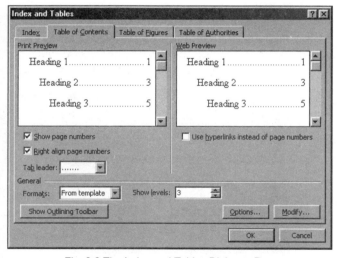

Fig. 8.6 The Index and Tables Dialogue Box

Pressing **OK** forms the table of contents shown in Fig. 8.7 on the next page. For a long document this can save you quite a lot of time, especially if you have to make editing changes which upset the document pagination.

Note that each line in the Table of Contents is now also a hyperlink to the corresponding heading in the document. To use these links you click the Table of Contents reference with the <Ctrl> key depressed.

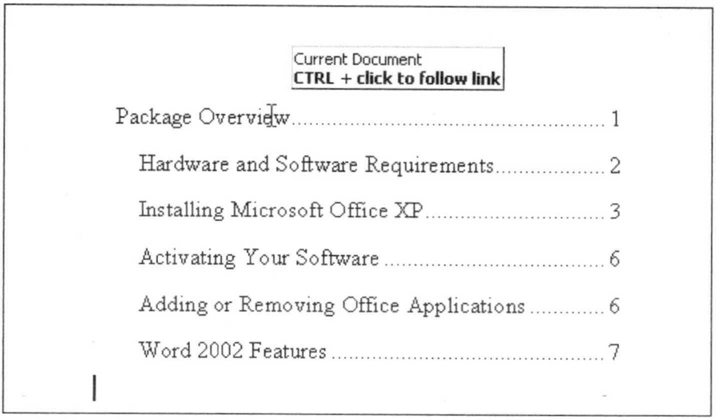

Current Document
**CTRL + click to follow link**

Fig. 8.7 A Simple Table of Contents

## Creating an Index

Before you can create an index, you must first mark all the text you want to appear in the index. To do this, click where you want to insert the index entry and press the <Alt+Shift+X> keys, to open the box shown in Fig. 8.8.

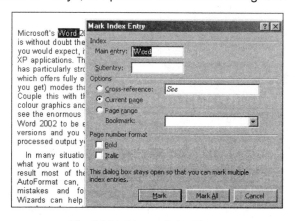

Fig. 8.8 Marking an Index Entry

To create the main index entry, type or edit the text in the **Main** **entry** box. You can customise the entry by creating a **Subentry** or by creating a cross-reference to another entry.

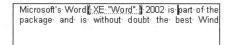

Fig. 8.9 An Inserted Index Code

When you click the **Mark** button an XE (Index Entry) field is added to your document, as shown here in Fig. 8.9. Word also sets your document to show all formatting characters. Work your way through the document marking all the entries you want. This can be quite a time consuming procedure, especially for a long document!

To create the index, click where you want to insert the finished index. Make sure that the document is paginated correctly by hiding field codes and hidden text. If the XE (Index Entry) fields are visible, click the **Show/Hide** button on the Standard toolbar. Use the **Insert**, **Reference**, **Index and Tables** command, and click the **Index** tab to open the following box.

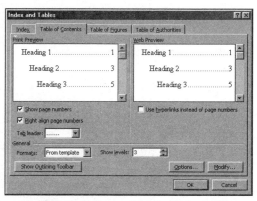

Fig. 8.10 The Index and Tables Dialogue Box

Select an index design from the **Formats** box or design your own custom index layout and click the **OK** button. To update the index, click to the left of the field and press **F9**.

# Assembling a Master Document

If you are involved in writing long 'documents', such as books, it is sometimes best if you split them into chapters, each having its own file. Anything above 20 to 30 pages gets very unwieldy and, particularly if it contains graphics, may strain your computer's resources.

If you have broken your long document (book) into smaller files (chapters) you can work with these separately until you need to print your work in its entirety, or create a table of contents or index showing the whole document page numbers. You can then create a 'Master Document'.

One method of doing this is to open a new document in Word, go into Outline View mode and type a document title. Next, on a new line press the **Insert Subdocument** button on the Outlining toolbar, shown here, then locate and select the file you want to insert into your Master Document from the Open dialogue box. This document is then inserted in your Master Document as shown in our example below.

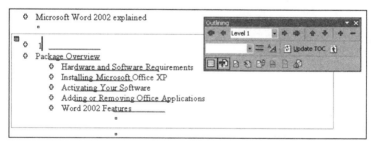

Fig. 8.11 A Master Document with an Inserted Subdocument

As can be seen in Fig. 8.11, the subdocument is placed in a 'section box' and a new ⊞ symbol has been added to the outline. You can drag this symbol around the outline screen to move the subdocument.

You can also add a new subdocument that does not have an existing file. To do this, place the insertion point on a new line of the master document and click the **Create**

**Subdocument** button (on the Outlining toolbar). Then type a heading for the subdocument, such as 'Chapter 2'. Use the buttons on the Outlining toolbar to promote or demote this entry to the same outline level as any other subdocument entries.

Save the master document with the **File**, **Save As** command in its own folder. Word automatically gives a file name to any newly created subdocuments based on the first characters in their heading in the master document outline. For example, a subdocument that begins with the outline heading 'Chapter 2' might be named 'Chapter 2.doc'

## Printing a Master Document

When you are finally ready to print the Master Document to paper, you can either print the entire document or specify the amount of detail you want to print.

To print the entire Master Document, click the **Expand Subdocuments** button, shown here, then switch to Print Layout view and print as usual. To specify the amount of detail you want to print, display the Master Document in Outline view, expand or collapse headings to display as much of the document as you require, then use the **File**, **Print** command.

# Scanning Documents

Office XP includes a Document Imaging program which can manage the separate tasks of controlling a scanner to scan text documents and then of performing optical character recognition (OCR) on them. If you have a scanner, this makes the task of getting printed text into your Word document very easy. It can save a lot of copy typing and in most cases Document Imaging can control the scanner software and carry out the OCR process without you having to do very much yourself.

Fig. 8.12 The Microsoft Office Tools

The Document Imaging and Scanning programs are self contained and are included in the Microsoft Office Tools which should have been installed on your PC with Office XP itself. You access them from the Windows **Start**, **Programs** cascading menu, as shown in Fig. 8.12. The Document Imaging option opens the larger window shown in Fig. 8.13.

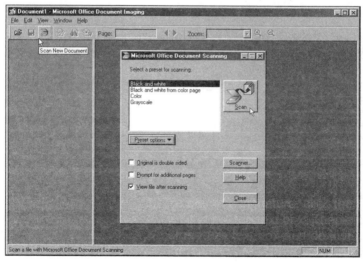

Fig. 8.13 The Document Imaging and Scanning Windows

The first time opened this will have two blank panes, as you will not have scanned any documents with the program. Clicking the **Scan New Document** button, pointed to above, opens the Document Scanning box shown in Fig. 8.13. This window is also opened straight away if you select the Document Scanning option from the menu in Fig. 8.12.

To scan a document, switch your scanner on, place the first page on the bed and click the large **<u>S</u>can** button on the Document Scanning window. From here on you simply follow any instructions that flash up. Document pages are scanned as **.tif** files and the OCR process is carried out automatically. Our example in Fig. 8.14 below shows the result of scanning the first draft page of Chapter 2 of this book.

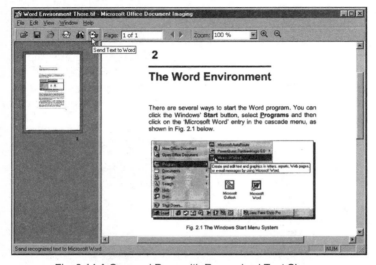

Fig. 8.14 A Scanned Page with Recognised Text Shown

Clicking the **Send Text to Word** button, pointed to above, does just that. This is a very easy to use program which makes scanning text into your word processor extremely easy.

To find out more detail, the **<u>H</u>elp** menu command opens the Document Imaging Help system, which is very good.

If you dig deeper, you will find that the OCR software included in this package is a 'cut-down' version and that you are entitled to upgrade to ScanSoft's OmniPage Pro OCR software at a special price. The full version does even cleverer things like maintaining the format of scanned text, and can even scan spreadsheet data.

# File Management

You can carry out most of your document management functions from the **Open** and **Save As** dialogue boxes. First, you locate the drive, folder and files with which you want to work in the **Look in** drop-down list. Then you can use right-click menus or the buttons displayed at the top of the Open dialogue box, shown annotated in Fig. 8.15 below.

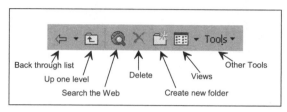

Fig. 8.15 The File Management Toolbar Buttons

When the file is found (you can even use wildcard characters in the **File name** box), select it in the **Look in** drop-down list then right-click it to display the shortcut menu shown in Fig. 8.16 below. This contains all the commands you should ever need to manage your documents.

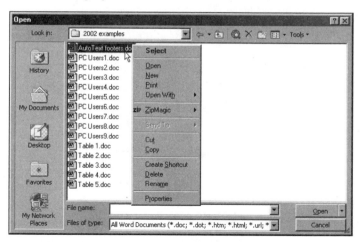

Fig. 8.16 A Right-click Context Menu for Managing Files

Clicking the **Views** button successively, rotates you through eight different displays of the listed sub-folders and files. These View options can also be selected from the **Views** drop-down menu shown in Fig. 8.17 below. Our example shows the **Pre<u>v</u>iew** option, which displays the selected document in a Preview box. As you select another file from the list, Word displays its contents too.

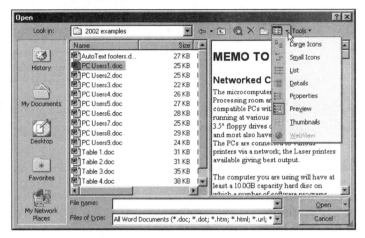

Fig. 8.17 The Views Options

The **Too<u>l</u>s** button provides additional options for working with files. A typical sub-menu of Tools options is shown in Fig. 8.18. Many of these are also available on the context menus that open when you right-click a listed file.

Fig. 8.18 The Tools Menu

# Compressing Pictures

Fig. 8.19 The Save As Tools Menu

As we have seen in an earlier chapter, Word is very good at handling graphic images in your documents. You can re-size and even edit them within Word itself. The only drawback to this is the enormous file sizes that can result. With previous versions of Word you had to live with this, but not any more.

With Word 2002, if you choose the **Save As** option and click the **Tools** button you will find the option to **Compress Pictures**, as shown here in Fig. 8.19.

Clicking this opens the Compress Pictures box shown in Fig. 8.20.

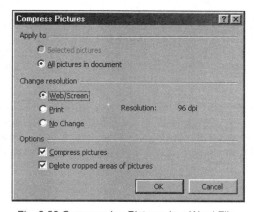

Fig. 8.20 Compressing Pictures in a Word File

Here you can choose to compress all the pictures in the document or only those actually selected. The **Web/Screen** option compresses pictures to a resolution of 96 dpi (dots per inch) which is the optimum for screen viewing. The **Print** option compresses to a resolution of 200 dpi, which is good enough for most print jobs. If you need to print at higher resolutions you should obviously **not** use these options.

## Places to Store Files

Both the Open and Save As dialogue boxes have a selection of icons down the left side to give instant access to particular file storage locations provided by Windows. Some comment is needed about some of these.

**My Documents folder** - This is the default saving and opening location, and is a good place to store files you are currently working on, such as documents, worksheets, or databases. (If you use Microsoft Windows NT Workstation 4.0, you can save files in the Personal folder.)

**Favorites folder** - A good place to store shortcuts to files and folders you use often, including those in remote network locations. The original file or folder does not move, but a shortcut that points to it is created. Storing shortcuts in the Favorites folder gives you quick access to any file without you having to remember where the file is located.

**My Network Places** - A good place to store files you want to copy or publish to folders on network file servers or Web servers. Saving files to a server allows others easy access to them.

This location appears in Windows 2000 and Windows Me. In Windows 98 and Windows NT 4.0, you use Network Neighborhood to work with files on network file servers, and Web Folders to work with files on Web servers.

# 9

# E-mail and Hyperlinks

Microsoft Word 2002, like its predecessor, has many design features built around the Internet, the main ones being its use as an e-mail editor and its ability to create and customise Web pages. Both of these features rely to a large extent on the ability to save any Word document as a fully editable HTML file.

## HTML File Format

Most Web pages are written in HTML (Hypertext Markup Language), which can be used by Web browsers on any operating system, such as Windows, Macintosh, and UNIX.

HTML pages are actually text documents which use short codes, or tags, to control text, designate graphical elements and hypertext links. Clicking a link on a Web page brings a document located on your hard disc, a local Intranet, or on a distant Internet server to your screen, irrespective of the server's geographic location. Documents may contain text, images, sounds, movies, or a combination of these, in other words - multimedia. All of these are 'built into' a Web page with HTML code.

E-mails created in Word 2002 can also use the HTML format. Most Windows application programs save their files, or data documents, in a proprietary binary format, which can only be read by the program itself. Word 2002, like earlier versions of Word, uses the .doc file format as the 'main' file saving format. Word documents can also be saved in HTML as an alternative file format, and the document can still be updated and edited using all of Word's extensive formatting tools.

This means that not only can Word 2002 documents now be published as 'instant' Web pages, but they can also be sent to other people, in a workgroup for example, who can read them in their Web browsers if they don't have a copy of Word on their computer. Microsoft Office has actually made HTML into a 'universal' file format, its application files being instantly readable by anyone with a normal Web browser.

To do this, extensive use is made of 'style sheets', and the downside is that the actual HTML code produced by Word is far too complex and convoluted for most Web authors to edit manually. Our example below shows only a quarter of the code produced for a document of only four lines of text. HTML documents produced this way can only really be edited in the original application itself.

```
p.MsoBodyText, li.MsoBodyText, div.MsoBodyText { mso-pagination: widow-orphan; fo
           font-family: Times New Roman; mso-fareast-font-family:
           Times New Roman; margin-left: 0cm; margin-right: 0cm;
           margin-top: 0cm; margin-bottom: .0001pt }
@page Section1
    {size:612.0pt 792.0pt;
    margin:72.0pt 90.0pt 72.0pt 90.0pt;
    mso-header-margin:36.0pt;
    mso-footer-margin:36.0pt;
    mso-paper-source:0;}
div.Section1 { page: Section1 }
-->
</style>
</head>

<body lang="EN-GB" style="tab-interval:36.0pt">

<div class="Section1">
   <p class="MsoBodyText"><b><i><span style="font-size:20.0pt;mso-bidi-font-size:
10.0pt">The Seagull<o:p></o:p></span></i></b></p>
   <p class="MsoBodyText"><span style="font-size:14.0pt;mso-bidi-font-size:10.0pt"
   seagull lies dead near the breaking waves.<b> </b>Stranded in death on the
   rocks and pebbles that lay strewn on the beach, each one appearing to me as a
   jewel of exquisite beauty.<span style="mso-spacerun: yes">  </span>The
   red coloured seaweed near the bird's head like a bloodstained pillow for its
   downy head. <o:p></o:p></span></p>
   <p class="MsoNormal"><![if !supportEmptyParas]> <![endif]><o:p></o:p></p>
</div>
<div style="mso-element:comment-list">
   <![if !supportAnnotations]>

   <hr class="msocomoff" align="left" size="1" width="33%">

   <![endif]>
</div>

</body>

</html>
```

In an effort to try to solve this problem, Word 2002 has a new filtered HTML output which removes the custom code needed to maintain the file's editability. This is available as a **Save as type** option from the **Save As** dialogue box.

Web pages saved in this format will no longer be editable in Word, but their file size is much smaller, which is important for Web transmissions. It is now much easier to use Word files, or parts of them, in other dedicated Web page development packages.

# E-mail

E-mail, or electronic mail, has to be one of the main uses of the Internet. It is very much faster that letter mail, known as 'snailmail' by many e-mail users. It consists of electronic text, that can be transmitted, sometimes in seconds, to anywhere else in the World that is connected to a main network. E-mail can also be used to send software and data files by attaching the files to a message.

There are many software packages dedicated to reading and sending e-mails, and we have probably tried most of them. Office XP comes bundled with Outlook 2002, Microsoft's latest e-mail and news editor. We find this an excellent program, especially as you can use Word to perform all the writing and editing of your e-mails. For more detail of using this package we suggest you try our book *Microsoft Office XP explained* (BP509), also published by Bernard Babani (publishing) Ltd. In what follows we assume you have installed Outlook and have it set up with the details of your e-mail Internet account.

# Word and Outlook 2002

If you use Outlook 2002 as your default mail client, you can use Word 2002 as your e-mail editor, instead of Outlook's much less powerful one. You can then create and edit your messages in Word using its extra features such as, automatic spelling, grammar checking, AutoCorrect, tables, the Document Map view, and the automatic conversion of e-mail names and Internet addresses into hyperlinks.

## Configuring Outlook for E-mail

If you need to configure Outlook 2002 to send and receive e-mail, open the program and use the **Tools**, **E-mail Accounts** menu command to open a series of dialogue boxes.

Select the **Add a new e-mail account** from the first box and press the **Next** button. In the next box select the type of e-mail server you have. With a telephone/modem connection this may well be **Pop3**, if not select the correct option and press the **Next** button to open the last box shown in Fig. 9.1 below.

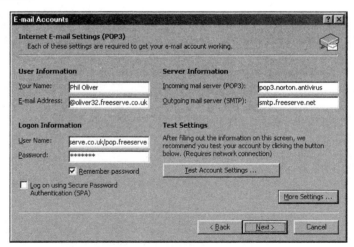

Fig. 9.1 Entering your E-mail Settings

- Type in **Your Name** and your **E-mail Address**. This is supplied to you by your Internet Service Provider, or ISP, when you join their service.

- Type in the name of the **Incoming mail server** and **Outgoing mail server**. Again these should be supplied to you by your ISP.

- Type in your **User name** and **Password** as supplied to you by your ISP.

- Test your entered settings if you like and click the final **Next** button.

If all is well, the final screen appears and you will be able to connect with the outside world.

Unless you have Outlook 2002 configured as your default e-mail program many of the e-mail features of Word 2002 will not work. A quick way to check this, is to look at the **E-mail** button on Word's Standard toolbar. If it is not 'active' and does not light up when you move the pointer over it, you should use the following procedure to set Outlook as your default e-mail program.

Click the Windows **Start** menu, followed by **Settings**, and **Control Panel**, then double-click on Internet Options to open the Internet Properties dialogue box shown here.

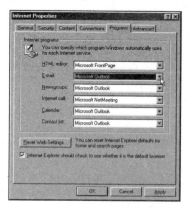

Fig. 9.2 Changing Internet Settings

Open the **Programs** tab sheet and select Microsoft Outlook
from the drop-down list in the **E-mail** box. Clicking **OK** will
confirm the new setting, but you will have to re-start your PC
for the change to actually take effect.

There is one other setting that may also need changing to
fully benefit from Word and its e-mail facilities. Open Outlook
2002, action the **Tools**, **Options** menu command, click the
**Mail Format** tab and make sure that the **Use Microsoft
Word to edit e-mail messages** option is selected.

# E-mailing a Document

There are often times when we are creating documents in
Word when we reach the stage that we want to send it to
someone else, maybe for comment, or approval. This is very
easy to do straight from Word 2002 itself. With the document

open in Word, you simply click the **E-mail** button, or
use the **File**, **Send To**, **Mail Recipient** command
sequence. These both open the e-mail header, shown
in Fig. 9.3 below, in which you control the e-mail posting.

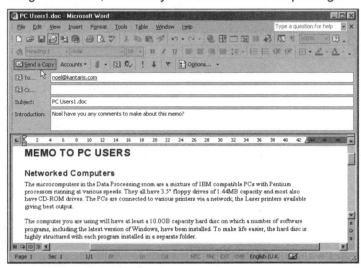

Fig. 9.3 Sending an E-mail from Word

Typing the e-mail address of your recipient in the **To** box, putting a brief message to them in the **Introduction** box and clicking the **Send a Copy** button is all you need to do. This sends the document to Outlook's Outbox. When it is actually transmitted will depend on your type of connection. With our Pop3 account, messages are only transmitted when we click the **Send/Receive** Outlook toolbar button. If you have a 'permanent', or Local Area Network, connection to the Internet, your messages should be transmitted straight away.

When you e-mail a document in this way, Word sends a copy of the document, and then closes the e-mail header. However, the original document stays open so that you can continue working on it if you want. When you save the document, the e-mail 'send' information is also saved with it. The next time you e-mail a copy of this document, the e-mail information

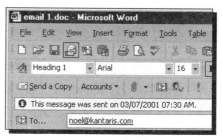

Fig. 9.4
E-mail Status Header

appears in the e-mail header, as shown here, making it easy to send further updates to the same recipients.

# Sending E-mail Messages

If you have set up to use Word as your e-mail editor, as described earlier, you still use Outlook to read your incoming messages, but whenever you click Outlook's **New** toolbar button to start a new e-mail message, a new Word window with the e-mail header bar, shown in Fig. 9.5 on the next page, will open for you.

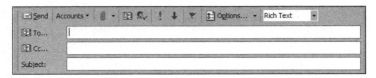

Fig. 9.5 Word's E-mail Header Bar

To start a new e-mail message straight from Word 2002, use the **File**, **New** menu command, and click the **Blank E-mail Message** option in the New Document Task Pane, as shown on page 16 in Fig. 2.2.

In the Word window that opens, you type the recipient's e-mail address in the **To** box, a title in the **Subject** box, and type your message, letter, memo, etc., in the main area, as shown in our example below.

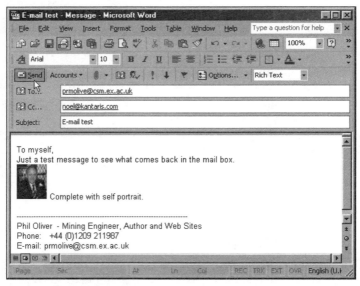

Fig. 9.6 Sending a Test Message

This message was actually sent from one of the authors to himself. A useful exercise when setting up a new e-mail facility, to test it without bothering anybody else! It also shows that you can include graphics in the message, and uses a 'signature' to automatically identify the sender.

When your message is to your complete satisfaction, you just click the **Send** button to send it to the Outlook Outbox. As before, when it is transmitted will depend on your settings in Outlook, but to send all the messages in the Outbox and download any new incoming mail from your server mail box, you can always click the **Send/Receive** button on the Outlook toolbar. The message box below tracks the progress of the sending operation.

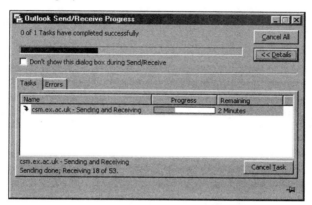

Fig. 9.7 E-mail Send/Receive Progress Tracker

In our case all was well and the message 'bounced' back almost immediately into the Outlook Inbox. If this does not happen for you, you will have to do some trouble shooting with Outlook's Options settings. Good luck!

## The E-mail Header Buttons

The buttons in Word's e-mail header control the settings of your messages and have the following functions:

      Send the e-mail message to the Outlook Outbox and close the Word window .

      Insert a file, or Outlook item, as an e-mail attachment.

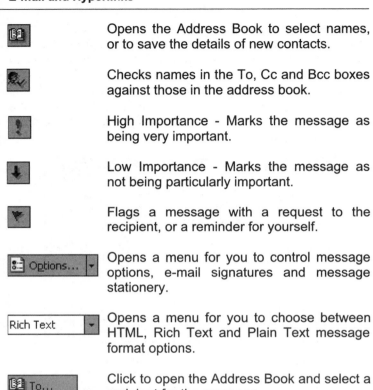

Opens the Address Book to select names, or to save the details of new contacts.

Checks names in the To, Cc and Bcc boxes against those in the address book.

High Importance - Marks the message as being very important.

Low Importance - Marks the message as not being particularly important.

Flags a message with a request to the recipient, or a reminder for yourself.

    Opens a menu for you to control message options, e-mail signatures and message stationery.

    Opens a menu for you to choose between HTML, Rich Text and Plain Text message format options.

Click to open the Address Book and select a recipient for the message.

Click to open the Address Book and select who should receive copies of the message.

Type a title for the e-mail message which will appear as a message header.

## Using Signatures

An e-mail signature consists of text that is automatically placed at the end of your messages. This usually consists of your name, address, phone number and your Web home page, but some people add lots more.

Word lets you create signatures and now provides an easier way to do it. You can still use the **Tools**, **Options** menu command, click the **General** tab, click the **E-mail Options** button, and then the **E-mail Signature** tab to finally open the E-mail Options dialogue box shown in Fig. 9.8 below. It is far easier though, to select the **E-mail Signature** option from the menu opened by clicking the **Options** button on the Word e-mail header bar.

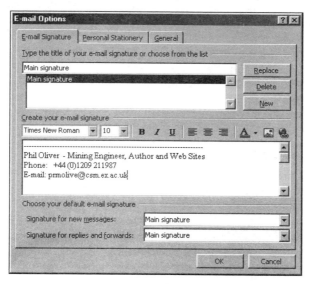

Fig. 9.8 Creating a New Signature

To create a signature, click the **New** button and type a name for it in the top text box. Then click in the **Create your e-mail signature** text box and do just that. The small toolbar above the editing area gives you plenty of control over the font and formatting of the signature text, and even has  buttons for adding pictures and hyperlinks. You could use the Insert Hyperlink icon, shown here, to point people towards your own Web site.

You can create different signatures for different types of messages. To make Word use one, by default, select it from the list in the **Signature for new messages** box.

Another method of placing your signatures might be using the **AutoText toolbar**. To open this bar, right-click on the Word toolbar and select it from the list of different toolbar options. Then when you have completed your message, place the cursor at the end, click the **All Entries** button and select which signature you want to use from the drop-down list, as shown here in Fig. 9.9. Once you have placed a signature on a

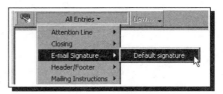

Fig. 9.9 Using the AutoText Toolbar

message, you can right-click in it and choose another (if you have created more) from the list menu that is opened. This is quite a powerful feature.

## Personalised Stationery

While the E-mail Options dialogue box is open it is well worth clicking the **Personal Stationery** tab, to open the box shown in Fig. 9.10 below.

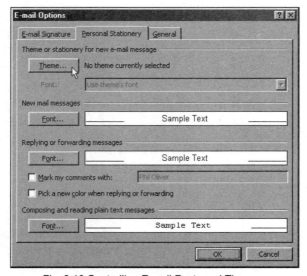

Fig. 9.10 Controlling E-mail Fonts and Themes

This lets you set what fonts and properties will be used for any new messages you send. Clicking the **Theme** button opens the box shown in Fig. 9.11 which offers some really spectacular e-mail formatting and background effects.

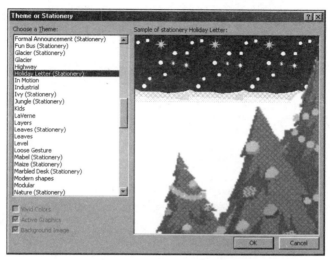

Fig. 9.11 Choosing a Stationery Theme for your E-mails

When you want to send a very special message, maybe like ours above at Christmas, you should be able to find a theme from the **Choose a Theme** list. We will leave it to you to experiment here.

Some of the options on the above list were not actually available to us, without having the original Office XP CD in its drive.

# Attaching a File

If you want to send a spreadsheet, Web page, or other type of file as an attachment to your main e-mail message you simply click the **Insert File** toolbar button. This opens the Insert File dialogue box, for you to select the file, or files, you want to go with your message.

Icons for the attached files are placed straight into the e-mail message itself, as shown in Fig. 9.12.

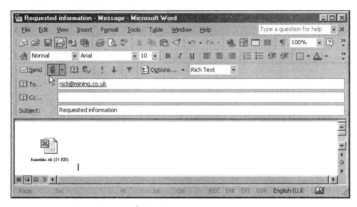

Fig. 9.12 An Attachment Placed in an E-mail

If you click the down-arrow next to the **Insert File** button and select the **Item** option the dialogue box of Fig. 9.13 opens. This lets you attach different types of Outlook items to your message.

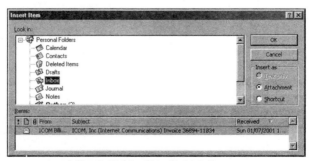

Fig. 9.13 Attaching Outlook Items

# The Address Book

Word has access to quite a useful series of address books which can make your e-mail life a little easier. To access them you click the **Address Book** button, shown here, or click on either the **To** or **Cc** buttons. All of these methods open the Select Names dialogue box below.

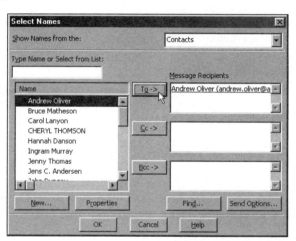

Fig. 9.14 Selecting from the Contacts Address Book

In this box you highlight a contact name in the left window, and click **To** if the main message is being sent to that contact, **Cc** if a copy is being sent to them, or **Bcc** for a blind copy. When the **OK** button is clicked the recipients' e-mail addresses are placed in the message header for you.

Like any address book though, it is only useful if kept up to date! To add a very comprehensive set of details of new friends or business contacts you click the **New** button. You can really go to town here, but don't forget the Data Protection Act!

That should be enough to get you going with Word 2002 as your e-mail editor. Very soon you should find that it becomes just an extension of your usual word processing.

# Using Hypertext Links

Hypertext links are elements in a document or Web page that you can click with your mouse, to 'jump to' another document. When clicked they actually fetch another file, or part of a file, to your screen, and the link is the address that uniquely identifies the location of the target file, whether it is located on your PC, on an Intranet, or on the Internet itself. This address is known as a Uniform Resource Locator (URL for short). For a link to an Internet file to work you must obviously have access to the Internet from your PC.

## Inserting a Hyperlink

If you know the URL address of the link destination, you can simply type it in a Word document and it will be automatically 'formatted' as a hyperlink by Word. This usually means it will change to bright blue underlined text. If you don't want to create hyperlinks, this feature can sometimes get annoying, but with Word 2002, you can turn it off if you want. Use the **Tools**, **AutoCorrect Options** menu command, click the **AutoFormat As You Type** tab and select or clear the **Internet and network paths with hyperlinks** check box.

In Word a hyperlink consists of the text , or image, that the user sees that describes the link, the URL of the link's target, and a ScreenTip (with an instruction) that appears whenever the pointer passes over the link on the screen.

To insert a hyperlink into Word, select the display text or image, and either use the **Insert, Hyperlink** command (<Ctrl+K>), or click the **Insert Hyperlink** button on the Standard toolbar, as shown here. Either action opens a dialogue box, shown in Fig. 9.15 on the next page, which allows you to browse for the destination address.

To illustrate the procedure, start Word, open the **PC Users4** memo, and highlight the word 'Explorer' to be found towards the end of it. Next, click the Hyperlink icon and locate the **explorer.exe** file (in the **Windows** folder) using the **Look in** list.

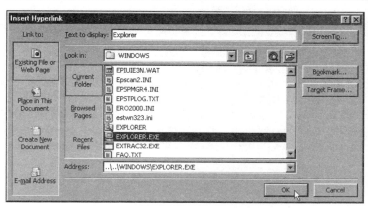

Fig. 9.15 Inserting a Hyperlink

Pressing the **OK** button, underlines the highlighted text and changes its colour to blue. When you point to such a hyperlink, a message opens, as shown here. We did not place a ScreenTip so the link address is shown instead. In our case, left-clicking the link with the <Ctrl> key depressed, starts the Explorer. When you have finished using the Explorer, click its **Close** button for the program to return you automatically to the hyperlinked Word document.

If the location of the file you wanted to hyperlink to is incorrect, or you did not highlight the word to be used as the hyperlink, then errors may occur. If that is the case, simply right-click the hyperlink and select the **Remove Hyperlink** option from the context menu.

## Inserting an Internet Hyperlink

To insert an Internet hyperlink into Word, select the display text or image, and click the **Insert Hyperlink** button to open the Insert Hyperlink dialogue box shown again in Fig. 9.16 on the next page.

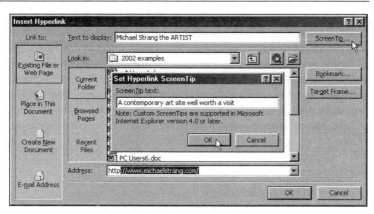

Fig. 9.16 Linking to a Web Page

To place an Internet hyperlink, click **Existing File or Web Page** on the 'Link to' bar and if necessary enter the hyperlink text in the **Text to display** box. Specify the linked document by either typing its URL in the **Address** box, as shown above, or choosing from the **Recent Files** or **Browsed Pages** file  lists. You could also click the **Browse the Web** button in the dialogue box and find the page to link to on the Internet.

Next, click **ScreenTip** to create a ScreenTip that will be displayed whenever the mouse pointer moves over the hyperlink. Clicking **OK** twice will place the link onto your document. Our example above placed the link shown here.

Fig. 9.17 A Hyperlink Screen Tip

Clicking this link with the <Ctrl> key depressed opened our Web browser, waited for us to connect to the Internet, loaded the linked Web site into it, and reduced the Word window to an icon on the Windows Task bar.

## Inserting Other Hyperlinks

There are three other types of hyperlinks you can place from the Insert Hyperlink box, shown by the other buttons on the **Link to** bar.

To link to a location in the same Word file, click the **Place in This Document** button. Before doing this, though, you should place a bookmark at the link location with the **Insert**, **Bookmark** command, so that you have somewhere to 'jump to'.

To link to a document not yet created, click the **Create New Document** button and enter the name for the new Word file. You can then edit the new file straight away or later on.

To create a link to an **E-mail Address**, either type the e-mail address you want in the **E-mail address** box, or select from the **Recently used e-mail addresses** box. In the **Subject** box, type the subject of the e-mail message. Some older browsers and e-mail programs may not recognise this subject line though.

Word will create a new e-mail message with the address already placed in the **To** line and a title in the **Subject** line of the message header, when the hyperlink is activated.

Word uses 'mailto' followed by the e-mail address and the subject line as the tip if you do not specify one. This type of link is usually used when you want to make it easy for people to contact you.

## Drag-and-drop Hyperlinks

You can also create a hyperlink by dragging selected text or a graphic from another Word document, a PowerPoint slide, a range in Excel, or a selected Access database object to your Word document. Both documents need to be saved as files before this will work.

To do this, open both files so that they are on the screen at the same time and select the text, graphic, or other item you want to jump to in the destination document.

Use the right mouse button to drag the selection to your document, release the mouse button and select **Create Hyperlink Here** from the shortcut menu, as shown here in Fig. 9.18.

Fig. 9.18 Creating a Drag and Drop Link

## Editing Hyperlinks

Once a hyperlink has been placed in a Word document it is very easy to change by right-clicking on it and selecting **Edit Hyperlink** from the drop-down menu. This opens a similar dialogue box to that used for inserting the link in the first place. You can make any changes you like in this box.

# 10

# Internet Web Pages

The World Wide Web, WWW, or Web as we shall call it, has been responsible for the rapidly expanding popularity of the Internet. When you see the Internet being accessed on TV, what you actually see is a Web page being read on a PC. A Web site is made up of a group of Web pages, all stored on an Internet server. The Web consists of many millions of such sites, located on server computers around the globe, all of which you can access with the browser on your PC.

So the Web consists of client computers (yours and mine) and server computers handling multimedia documents with hypertext links built into them (Web pages). Client computers use browser software (such as Internet Explorer and Navigator) to view pages of these documents, one at a time. Server computers use Web server software to maintain the documents for the rest of us to access.

Earlier with the introduction of Word 2000, Microsoft went one step nearer making it possible for anyone to very easily prepare their own Web pages and keep them up to date on their own Internet Web site. This was done largely with the introduction of Web Folders (now My Network Places with Windows Me) which, once set up, formed shortcuts to the Web servers where Internet Web files are stored. This is still a new concept, and unfortunately at the time of writing, our own ISPs had no facilities to support Web Folders.

We do not have the space here to fully cover web site design and management, we can only introduce some of Word's useful features. If you want more detail on Web sites generally, may we suggest you read our book *Your own Web site on the Internet* (BP433), also published by Bernard Babani (publishing) Ltd.

# Creating Web Pages

You can use Word 2002 to create a Web page in the same way you create a 'regular' Word document, by simply saving it as an HTML file, but Word also offers other easy ways to begin Web pages.

## Using an Existing Word Document

If you are happy using Word, you can use it to do all your Web editing. The example below is an opening page for a Web site prepared as a normal **.doc** file in Word.

Fig. 10.1 A Web Page Created in Word

Note that it is shown in Web Layout View, controlled by the buttons on the bottom scroll bar. With this view, Word attempts to show the document as it will appear on the Web. To get an even better idea, you can also use the **File**, **Web Page Preview** command to see the file opened in Internet Explorer, or your default Web browser.

You save an existing, or newly created, document as a Web page with the **File**, **Save as Web Page** menu command. If you want to save the document in a different folder, locate and open the folder and in the **File name** box, type a name for the Web page. While the Save As box is open, as shown below, click the **Change Title** button and type the title you want to appear in the titlebar of the browser when the page is viewed. Click **OK** and then the **Save** button to complete the saving process.

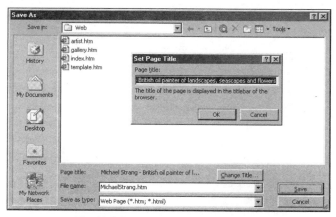

Fig. 10.2 Saving a File as a Web Page

When you save a document as a Web page, all its graphics and objects, such as pictures, AutoShapes, WordArt, text boxes, Equation Editor objects, Organization Chart objects, and Graph objects, are saved as **.gif**, **.jpg**, or **.png** files, so that they can be viewed in a Web browser. When you later reopen the Web page in Microsoft Word, the graphics and objects you see are in their original formats so that you can edit them as normal. Very clever stuff this!

## Using the Web Page Wizard

By using the Web Page Wizard, you can create a single Web page or an entire Web site. You can add existing Web pages to your Web site, add a theme and even use frames to improve the look of your Web pages.

To open the Wizard, use the **F**i**le**, **N**e**w** menu command, select **General Templates** from the New Document Task Pane, click the **Web Pages** tab and double-click the **Web Page Wizard** icon shown here.

The opening screen of this Wizard is shown in Fig. 10.3 below. You really must spend a few minutes exploring this feature, it is the best method we have seen so far for easily building Web sites. Amazingly it even lets you use frames, which can be quite tricky to get right.

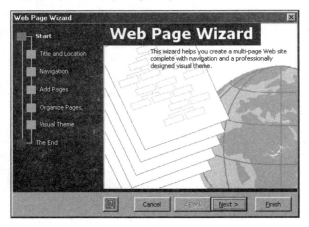

Fig. 10.3 The Web Page Wizard

Once you click the **F**i**nish** button to close the Wizard, the opening page of your new Web site is opened as a Word document for you to edit and customise to your heart's content.

## Using a Web Page Template

When you use a Web page template, Word can make features that are not supported by your target browser unavailable so that you can design impressive Web pages without having to worry about how your formatting will look in a Web browser. You can change your target browser or turn the browser setting off, add a theme and use frames to make your Web pages more dynamic.

Selecting **General Templates** from the New Document Task Pane opens the Templates dialogue box shown below with the Web Pages tab selected.

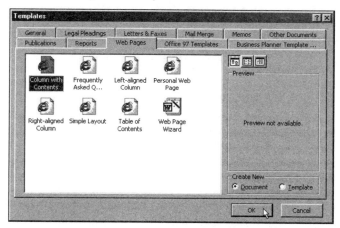

Fig. 10.4 Available Web Page Templates

This shows the seven Web page templates that were available to us. Double-clicking a template icon opens an HTML Word document, as shown below. You then have to customise this page with your own contents. Have fun.

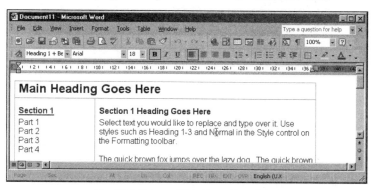

Fig. 10.5 Using a Web Page Template

To turn features on or off that are not supported by some Web browsers use the **Tools**, **Options**, menu command, click the **General** tab, followed by **Web Options**, and then click the **Browsers** tab. We suggest you select the **Disable features not supported by these browsers** check box and in the **People who use this Web page will be using:** box, choose 'Microsoft Internet Explorer 4.0 and Netscape Navigator 4.0 or later'. Your pages should then work with most Web browsers used.

## Adding a Theme to a Page

As well as the Wizard and templates, Word has a collection of Web page themes that give you a variety of standard page designs, which control the page background, fonts, and colours used in the Web page. You can actually select a theme in the Web Page Wizard, but you can also select one from your Word document. To see some of the effects though, you will have to be in Web Page view. To select a theme, use the **Format**, **Theme** menu command, which opens the following dialogue box.

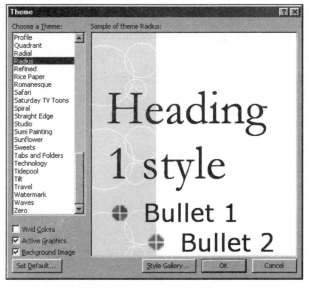

Fig. 10.6 A Selection of Word Themes

As you work your way down the list of themes, a sample of each is displayed in the right-hand window pane. The **Style Gallery** option is not of much use for Web pages, but if you find a theme you like you can click the **Set** **D**efault button to have it used for all your new Web pages.

The **Vivid** **C**olors option makes some of the theme colours even more garish, **Active** **G**raphics lets you turn on, or off, any moving graphics in the theme, and **Background Image** controls whether you have a theme image or a plain colour as the page background.

## Adding Movies and Sounds

With Word 2002 it is easy to add special effects to your Web pages, such as movies or sounds. We don't really recommend it, but you can add an in-line movie, which will be downloaded and played when the page is opened. If you don't want the movie to play whenever the page is opened, you can insert a hyperlink to the movie file, which will then only be downloaded and played when the link is clicked.

To add a background movie, or sound, open the Web Tools toolbar, shown here, click the **Movie** or **Sound** button and enter the path or Web address of the movie or sound file you want, or click **Bro**w**se** to locate the file.

For a sound file, enter the number of times you want the background sound to repeat, in the **Loop** box.

To be able to hear background sound, a user must have a sound card installed on their computer and their Web browser must support the sound format of the file used. The types of sound files that can be used this way include, **.wav**, **.mid**, **.au**, **.aif**, **.rmi**, **.snd**, and **.mp2** (MPEG audio) formats.

The last icon in the Web Tools bar lets you place scrolling text on your page. This can sometimes be useful, but more often is just a distraction! Most of the other Web Tools buttons are to help you build Web page forms.

# Some HTML Differences

As we have seen, Word 2002 automatically converts Word's **.doc** file format to HTML when creating Web pages, and back to **.doc** format when the files are loaded into the word processor. This conversion process is fairly accurate, but by no means perfect because of the basic restrictions inherent in HTML.

With HTML you cannot embed fonts and you have to use tables to control the layout of complex pages. Without them HTML will not let you simulate multiple column layouts, or very specific spacings of text blocks.

Because Word provides formatting options far more powerful than that of most Web browsers, some text and graphics may look different when you view them on a Web page. We suggest that when creating documents for the Web with Word you use the Web Layout view from scratch. This will help to ensure that your graphics look the way you want them to when they are viewed as Web pages in a Web browser.

# Saving Web Pages on the Internet

With Windows NT 4.0 or Windows 98 you can use Web Folders, but with Windows 2000 or Windows Me these are called My Network Places. If you are lucky and your Web server supports Web Folders / My Network Places you can use them to save copies of your Web pages to the Web server. Before trying to save and manage folders and files on a Web server, you should contact your system administrator or Internet Service Provider (ISP) to get access and find out the URL, or Web address, you should use.

If your Web server supports File Transfer Protocol (FTP), and most do, you can save or upload your Web pages to an FTP site. Before you try to use FTP, contact your system administrator or ISP to get access details of the location you can save your files to.

## Web Folders / My Network Places

These are shortcuts to a Web server, and let you very easily publish documents for viewing in Web browsers. To use them, the Web server must support Microsoft SharePoint Portal Server and unfortunately ours does not seem to. Hopefully, given time, most ISPs will provide this support.

If you find you can use Web folders / My Network Places, you must first add one to your system. In Word 2002, we used **File**, **Open**, clicked the **My Network Places** button and then double-clicked the **Add Network Place** icon, as shown below, to start the Add Network Place Wizard.

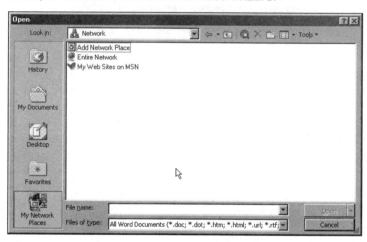

Fig. 10.7 Working with My Network Places / Web Folders

Complete the Wizard with the details you obtained from your System Administrator, and as long as you are connected to the Internet a new folder should be placed in your Web Folders / My Network Places section.

Once you have added a Web Folder / My Network Place, you can save your Web files and other sub-folders to that location on the Internet server in exactly the same way as you save a file to your hard disc. You must of course be connected to the Internet at the time.

# Uploading to an FTP Site

Even if your Web server does not support Web Folders / My Network Places, it certainly should let you have FTP access to your Web space on the server. Once you have the access details from your System Administrator and before you can save any files to an FTP site with Word, you must add the site to the list of Internet sites on your PC. With Word open, click the **Open** button on the Standard toolbar, and in the **Look in** box, click **Add/Modify FTP Locations**, to open the dialogue box shown below.

Fig. 10.8 Adding an FTP Location

In the **Name of FTP site** box, type the FTP site name given to you by your ISP. This could be a series of numbers separated by dots, or a URL. If you have user privileges for the site, click **User**, and enter your UserID and your password, and click **Add**. When you have finished here click the **OK** button.

To save a Web page file from Word to your FTP site, and hence make it available over the Internet, first make sure your Internet connection is open. Then use the **File**, **Save As** command and in the **Save in** box, double-click the FTP site you want, as shown in Fig. 10.9 below.

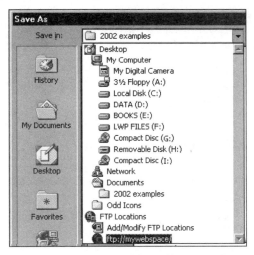

Fig. 10.9 Saving a File to an FTP Location

This should make the connection to your Web server space, and present you with the list of folders and files that are there. Double-click the location at the site you want, type the document name and click the **Save** button to, hopefully, complete the operation.

In the future, if you need to edit or update a Web page, you can use the Open dialogue box to retrieve the file from your Web server. Once you have carried out your work you can save it back again as described above.

## Supporting Files

When you save Web page files from Word 2002 to a Web server or a location on your hard disc, all their supporting files, such as graphics, bullets and background images are, by default, placed in a supporting folder. If you move or copy your Web page to another location, you must also move the supporting folder so that you maintain all links to your Web page.

As an example, if you save a Web page called **Page1.htm**, its bullets and other graphic files would be stored in a 'supporting files' folder called **Page1_files**. So if you move the file **Page1.htm**, you must also move the supporting files folder **Page1_files** to the new location.

By default, the name of the supporting folder is the name of the Web page plus an underscore (_), a period (.), or a hyphen (-), followed by the word 'files'.

## Web Archive Files

You can also save your Web page as a Web archive (MHTML) file so that all the text and graphics are stored embedded in a single file. To do this, select 'Web Archive' as the **Save as type** in the Save As dialogue box, as shown in Fig. 10.10 below.

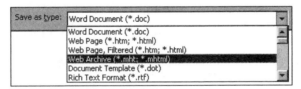

Fig. 10.10 Saving a Document as a Web Archive File

You can move or send the MHTML archive file as an e-mail attachment without worrying about broken links. You can view this type of file with Internet Explorer 4.0 and later.

# 11

## Sharing Information

You can link or embed all or part of an existing file created either in an Office application or in any other application that supports Object Linking and Embedding (OLE). However, if an application does not support OLE, then you must use the copy/cut and paste commands to copy or move information from one application to another. In general, you copy, move, link, embed, or hyperlink information depending on the imposed situation, as follows:

| Imposed Situation | Method to Adopt |
|---|---|
| Inserted information will not need updating, or Application does not support OLE. | Copy or move |
| Inserted information needs to be automatically updated in the destination file as changes are made to the data in the source file, or Source file will always be available and you want to minimise the size of the destination file, or Source file is to be shared amongst several users. | Link |
| Inserted information might need to be updated but source file might not be always accessible, or Destination file needs to be edited without having these changes reflected in the source file. | Embed |
| To jump to a location in a document or Web page, or to a file that was created in a different program. | Hyperlink |

# Copying or Moving Information

To copy or move information between programs running under Windows, such as Microsoft applications, is extremely easy. To move information, use the drag and drop facility, while to copy information, use the **Edit, Copy** and **Edit, Paste** commands.

To illustrate the technique, you will need to either create an Excel file, or have such a file on disc. We will copy into Word our previously created Excel file **Project3.xls**, considering the following two possibilities:

## Source File Available without Application

Let us assume that you only have the source file **Project3.xls** on disc, but not the application that created it (that is you don't have Excel). In such a situation, you can only copy the contents of the whole file to the destination (in our case Word). To achieve this, do the following:

Start Word and minimise it on the Taskbar. Use My Computer (or Explorer) to locate the file whose contents you want to copy into Word.

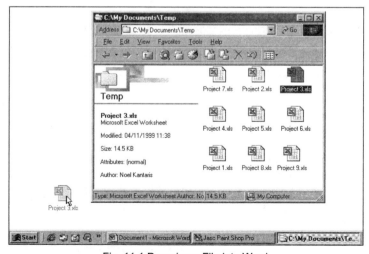

Fig. 11.1 Dragging a File into Word

Click the filename that you want to copy, hold the mouse button down and drag the pointer, as shown in Fig. 11.1, until it is over Word on the Taskbar. Hold it there until the Word window opens.

With the mouse button still held down, move the mouse pointer into Word's open document to the point where you want to insert the contents of the file, in our case **Project3.xls**. Releasing the mouse button will place the contents of **Project3.xls** into Word at that point.

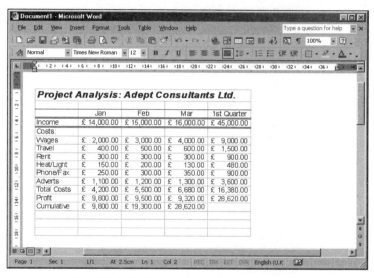

Fig. 11.2 A Small Spreadsheet Copied into Word

What you have actually done here, is created a 'spreadsheet object' in your Word document. To move it, you have to right-click in the copied sheet and select **Format Object** from the context menu. Select the wrapping style from the Format Object dialogue box as discussed in an earlier chapter. This is important, as by default an inserted object is placed **In line with text** and unless you change this you will not be able to move it around your document.

## Source File and Application Available

Assuming that you have both the file and the application that created it on your computer (which should be the case if you have installed Office XP), you can copy all or part of the contents of the source file to the destination file.

Start Excel, open **Project3.xls**, highlight only the information that you want to copy and click the **Copy** icon on the toolbar, as shown in Fig. 11.3 below.

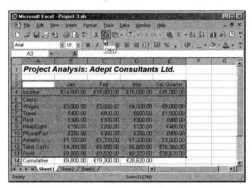

Fig. 11.3 Copying a Selection from Excel

Start Word and click the Paste Cells icon on the toolbar.

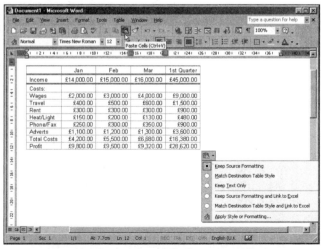

Fig. 11.4 Spreadsheet Cells Pasted into Word

Fig. 11.4 also shows a new feature incorporated into Word 2002, the **Paste Options** Smart Tag button. In our example we have clicked it to open a menu of very relevant formatting and linking options. You can select from this menu, or just carry on with your work, and it will go away.

# Insert an Excel Worksheet in Word

If the **Insert Microsoft Excel Worksheet** button, shown here, appears on your Word Standard toolbar, you can use it to insert an empty worksheet of the required number of rows and columns, by simply clicking the button and dragging down to the right. As you drag the mouse, the **Worksheet** button expands to create the grid of rows and columns, shown in Fig. 11.5 below, in a similar manner to that of creating rows and columns of tables.

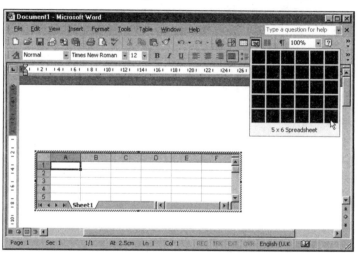

Fig. 11.5 Inserting a New Excel Worksheet into a Document

When you release the mouse button, the worksheet is inserted in your Word document. You can then insert data and apply all of Excel's functions to them. To find out more on these we suggest our book *Microsoft Excel 2002 explained* (BP511) in the same series.

# Object Linking and Embedding

Object Linking is copying information from one file (the source file) to another file (the destination file) and maintaining a connection between the two files. When information in the source file is changed, then the information in the destination file is automatically updated. Linked data is stored in the source file, while the file into which you place the data stores only the location of the source and displays a representation of the linked data.

For example, you would use Object Linking if you would want an Excel chart included in, say, a Word document to be updated whenever you changed the information used to create the chart in the first place within Excel. In such a case, the Excel worksheet containing the chart would be referred to as the source file, while the Word document would be referred to as the destination file.

Object Embedding is inserting information created in one file (the source file) into another file (the container file). After such information has been embedded, the object becomes part of the container file. When you double-click an embedded object, it opens in the application in which it was created in the first place. You can then edit it in place, and the original object in the source application remains unchanged.

Thus, the main differences between linking and embedding are where the data is stored and how it is updated after you place it in your file. Linking saves you disc space as only one copy of the linked object is kept on disc. Embedding a logo chosen for your headed paper, saves the logo with every saved letter!

In what follows, we will discuss how you can link or embed either an entire file or selected information from an existing file, and how you can edit an embedded object. Furthermore, we will examine how to mail merge a letter written in Word with a list created either in Access, Excel, Outlook, or even Word itself.

## Linking or Embedding an Existing File

To embed an existing file in its entirety into another application, do the following:

- Open the container file, say Word, and click where you want to embed the file.

- Use the **Insert, Object** command, to open the Object dialogue box, shown below, when the **Create from File** tab is clicked.

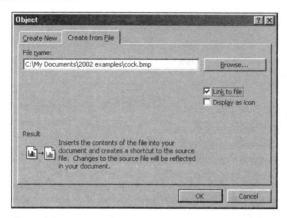

Fig. 11.6  Linking a Graphics File to a Word Document

To locate the file you want to link or embed, click **Browse**, and then select the options you want.

- In the **File name** box, you can type the name of the file you want to link or embed.

- To maintain a link to the original file, check the **Link to file** box.

**Note:** To insert graphics files that you will not want to edit from Word it is easier to use the **Insert, Picture, From File** command instead of the **Insert, Object** command. This displays the Insert Picture dialogue box which allows you to specify within the **Look in** box the folder and file you want to insert.

## Linking or Embedding Selected Information

To link or embed selected information from an existing file created in one application into another, do the following:

* Select the information in the source file you want to link or embed.

* Use the **Edit, Copy** command to copy the selected information to the Clipboard.

* Switch to the container file or document in which you want to place the information, and then click where you want the information to appear.

* Use the **Edit, Paste Special** command to open the following dialogue box:

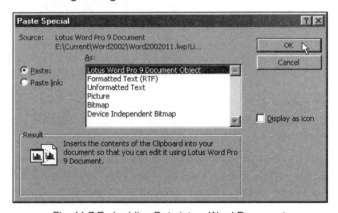

Fig. 11.7 Embedding Data into a Word Document

* To link the information, click the **Paste link** radio button, or to embed the information, click the **Paste** radio button, as shown in Fig. 11.7 above. In the **As** box, click the item with the word 'Object' in its name. For example, if you copied the information from a Lotus Word Pro document, as we have for this example, the Lotus Word Pro 9 Document Object appears in the **As** box. Select this object and press **OK**.

## Editing an Embedded Object

If the application in which you created an embedded object is installed on your computer, double-click the object to open it for editing. Some applications start the original application in a separate window and then open the object for editing, while other applications temporarily replace the menus and toolbars in the current application so that you can edit the embedded object in place, without switching to another window.

If the application in which an embedded object was created is not installed on your computer, convert the object to the file format of an application you do have. For example, if your Word document contains an embedded Microsoft Works Spreadsheet object and you do not have Works, you can convert the object to an Excel Workbook format and edit it in Excel.

Some embedded objects, such as sound and video clips, when double-clicked start playing their contents, instead of opening an application for editing. To illustrate this, we copied an .avi video file into a Word document using the **Copy, Paste Special** command (we also clicked the **Paste** radio button and the **Display as icon** box on the displayed dialogue box).

 This placed a Windows Media Player icon in the document, as shown here. Double-clicking such an icon, starts the video playing.

To edit one of these objects, select it and use the **Edit {Video Clip Object}, Edit** command. What appears inside the curly brackets here, depends on the selected object; video clip in this case. In our case this opened the Media Player Video Clip Editor shown in Fig. 11.8 below.

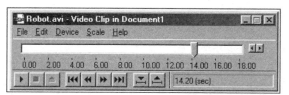

Fig. 11.8 Windows Media Player Video Clip Editor

# How To Mail Merge

There are times when you may want to send the same basic letter to several different people, or companies. The easiest way to do this is with a Mail Merge operation. Two files are prepared; a 'Data source' file with the names and addresses, and a 'main document' file, containing the text and format of the letter. The two files are then merged together to produce individual letters to each party listed in the original data file.

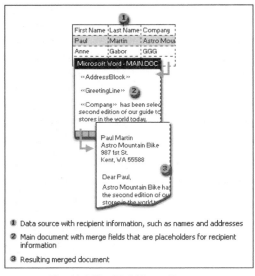

Fig. 11.9 The Mail Merge Process

With Word 2002, Microsoft have given a lot of thought to making this operation much more intuitive, and have come up with a Task Pane based Wizard. It is both easy to access, and with a little patience is very easy to use.

Before creating a list of names and addresses for a mail merge, you need to select the Office application that is most suited to the task. For a mail merge, you can use a list you create in Access, Excel, Outlook, or Microsoft Word itself.

- For a long list in which you expect to add, change, or delete records, and for which you want powerful sorting and searching capabilities at your disposal, you should think of using Microsoft Access, then specify the appropriate data file in the mail Merge operation.

- You can select to use the list of names and addresses in your Outlook Contact List.

- For a small to medium size list of names and addresses in which you do not expect to make too many changes, you could create your data list in Word 2002 itself. This facility is quite powerful now.

We will illustrate the mail merge procedure by using a memo created in Word (**PC Users1**) and a table which is created in Word, but it could easily already exist either as an Outlook Contacts address book, or in an Access table.

No matter which method you choose, first start Word and open the **PC Users1** memo (or your own letter), place three empty lines at the very top of the memo/letter and choose the Normal paragraph style for them.

Next, select **Tools**, **Letters & Mailings**, **Mail Merge Wizard** which displays the Mail Merge Task Pane shown in Fig. 11.10 below.

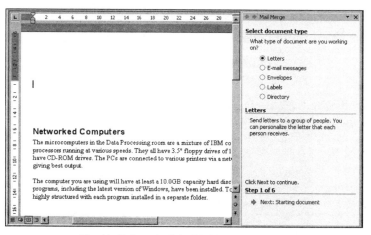

Fig. 11.10 Step 1 of the Mail Merge Process

With Letters selected as the type of document to use, click on **Next: Starting document** at the bottom of the pane.

In the next pane elect to **Use the current document**. This will let us add fields to the memo to form the basis of the merge documents. Click on **Next: Select Recipients** to open Step 3 of the Wizard shown in Fig. 11.11.

Fig. 11.11 Mail Merge Step 3

It is here that you can select either to use an existing list of addresses (which might be found in either Word, Excel, Access, etc.), to use a list of contacts in one of the electronic address books in Outlook, or to type a new list in Word 2002 itself.

In what follows, we will step through the procedure of creating a new data list in Word itself. You can, of course, use one of the other two options if you already have an existing data list.

## Creating an Address List in Word

Selecting **Create**, displays the following dialogue box.

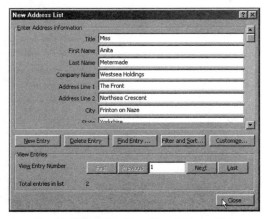

Fig. 11.12 Building Up a New Address List

As you can see, Word provides commonly used field names for your address list. Selecting the **Customize** button lets you add new field names, delete unwanted ones, rename them, or move them up or down the list.

When you are happy with the field names for your list, carry on and enter the data for each person or company. Press the **New Entry** button to record each complete field entry. Pressing the **Close** button displays a Save As dialogue box, in which you can name your data list, say **Address**. Word automatically adds the file extension **.mdb**, saves the data file as an Access database and opens it as shown below in Fig. 11.13.

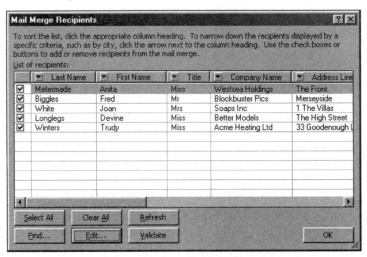

Fig. 11.13 The Mail Merge Recipients Database

Here you can edit the list and sort it on any of its fields. We have typed in several fictitious entries in order to demonstrate the process, but we have not attempted to change the field names provided in any way whatsoever.

You control which entries from the data list are included in your mail merge by placing a tick ☑ in the left hand box, either manually or by manipulating the list and clicking the **Select All** button. When finished here, press the **OK** button, followed by the **Next: Write your letter** Task Pane link.

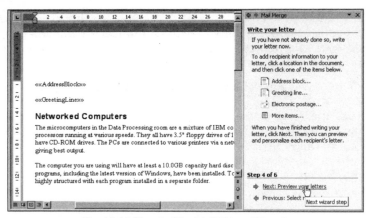

Fig. 11.14 Step 4 of the Mail Merge Wizard

Fig. 11.14 actually shows the **Write your letter** Task Pane with the completed letter ready for the merge on the left. With this Task Pane open you can write or edit the letter. In our case we want to put an address at the top of each letter, followed by the greeting line, as shown above.

To do this, we placed the insertion point on the top line of the letter, and clicked the **Address block** link in the Task Pane. This opened the dialogue box below.

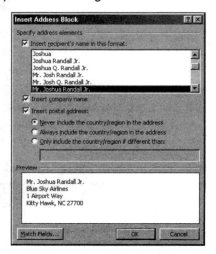

Fig. 11.15 Insertion Details for the Address Block

In this box you can arrange which fields you want included in the letter address and their layout. We accepted the defaults, clicked the **OK** button and then clicked the **Greeting Line** link, to open the box shown next in Fig. 11.16.

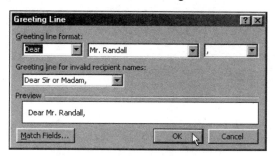

Fig. 11.16 Controlling the Greeting Line Format

Again we accepted the defaults, but you can make any changes you want here. When you are happy, click the **Next: Preview your letters** link pointed to in Fig. 11.14 to see what your final letters will look like (Fig. 11.17).

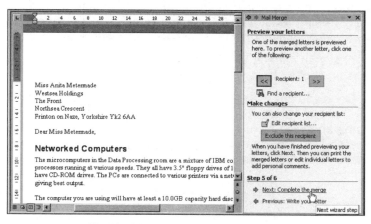

Fig. 11.17 Previewing the Merged Letters

You can step between the letters here, to check who will receive them, or exclude particular recipients from the mail merge. When you are finally ready, clicking the **Next: Complete the merge** link will open the final pane in the Wizard, shown in Fig. 11.18 on the next page.

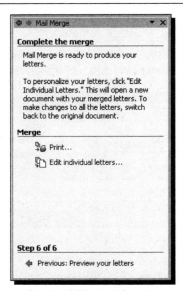

Fig. 11.18 The Last Stage!

At this stage a merge document has been created with all the letters being ready to print. All that remains to be done is to **Print** your 'mailshot', or to personalise any letters you want.

That's all there is to it. You will possibly find it takes much less time to do, than to read about it!

Once you have used the Wizard a few times you may want to 'handle' your mail merges yourself. There is a very comprehensive toolbar, shown floating in Fig. 11.19, to help you do just that. By now you should be able to find your way round its features yourself.

Fig. 11.19 The Mail Merge Toolbar

# 12

# Customising Word 2002

## Word Macro Basics

A macro is simply a set of instructions made up of a sequence of keystrokes, mouse selections, or commands stored in a macro file. After saving, or writing, a macro and attaching a quick key combination to it, you can run the same sequence of commands whenever you want. This can save a lot of time and, especially with repetitive operations, can save mistakes creeping into your work.

In Word there are two basic ways of creating macros. The first one is generated by the program itself, recording and saving a series of keystrokes, or mouse clicks. The second one involves using Visual Basic for Applications, the programming language that is common to all Office XP applications. With this method, you can write quite complex macro programs directly into a macro file using the Visual Basic Editor.

### Recording a Macro

To demonstrate how easy it is to save and name a macro, we will start with a simplistic one that enhances the word at the cursor to bold italics type. Open **PC Users1**, place the cursor in a document word and either double-click the **REC** indicator on the Status bar, shown below, or select the **Tools**, **Macro**, **Record New Macro** command.

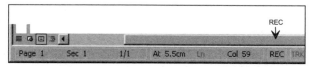

Fig. 12.1 The Macro Indicator on the Status Bar

Either of these, opens the Record Macro dialogue box shown
in Fig. 12.2. In the **Macro name** input box, type a name for
your macro (call it BoldItalic), then give your macro a
**Description** (such as Bold & Italic) and click on the
**Keyboard** button.

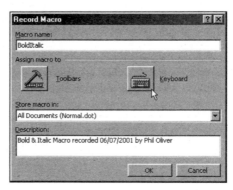

Fig. 12.2 The Record Macro Dialogue Box

In the displayed Customize Keyboard dialogue box, shown in
Fig. 12.3, press a suitable key stroke combination, such as
<Ctrl+Shift+I>, in the **Press new shortcut key** input box.

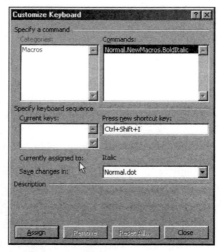

Fig. 12.3 Adding Keyboard Commands to a Macro

You will be informed whether this key combination is currently attached to an internal macro or not, as shown in Fig. 12.3.

Most <Ctrl>, or <Shift> keys with a letter or function key combinations are suitable (the word [unassigned] will appear under the **Currently assigned to:** heading) if the chosen combination of keys is not already assigned to a macro. Our choice of key strokes results in the message 'Italic', under the **Currently assigned to:** heading. This does not matter in this instance, because both the key combinations <Ctrl+I> and <Ctrl+Shift+I> are assigned to Italic, so we can use one.

Next, press the **Assign** button followed by the **Close** button. From this point on, all key strokes and mouse control clicks (but not mouse movements in the editing area) will be recorded. To indicate that the recorder is on, Word attaches a recorder graphic to the mouse pointer, as shown here. Word also displays the **Stop** and **Pause** buttons to allow you to stop or pause a macro.

A macro can also be stopped by double-clicking at the **REC** button on the Status bar.

While the cursor is still placed in the word to be modified, use the key strokes, <Ctrl+⇨> to move to the end of the current word followed by <Shift+Ctrl+⇦> to highlight it, click the **Bold** and **Italic** buttons on the Formatting toolbar, press the <⇨> key to cancel the highlight and click the **Stop** button on the Macro Record toolbar. Your macro should now be recorded and held in memory.

By default your macros will be incorporated into Word's Normal template, so that you can use them in any documents created at a later date. To restrict a macro to the current document only you should select the document filename in the **Store macro in** box of the Record Macro dialogue box (Fig. 12.2).

**Please note:** If your PC is Virus protected, particularly by a program that stops macros writing to your hard disc, you may have to disable it before you can save macros.

## Playing Back a Macro

There are four main ways of running a macro. You can use the playback shortcut keys straight from the keyboard; in our case place the cursor in another word and press the <Ctrl+Shift+I> keys. The word should be enhanced automatically. If not, check back that you carried out the instructions correctly.

The second method is to select the **Tools**, **Macro**, **Macros** command, or the <Alt+**F8**> keyboard shortcut, then select the macro from the list, as shown below, and press the **Run** button.

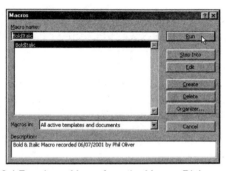

Fig. 12.4 Running a Macro from the Macros Dialogue Box

From this dialogue box you can also **Edit**, **Create** or **Delete** macros, or select the **Organizer** which allows you to copy macro sets between the document and the Normal template.

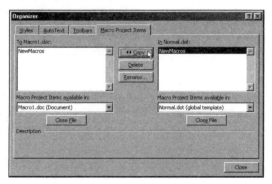

Fig. 12.5 Organising Macro Sets

## Attaching Macros/Commands to a Toolbar

The last two methods of activating a macro are to attach it to a custom button on a toolbar or to add it to a menu, and simply click the button or the menu option.

To assign a macro to a toolbar, use the **Tools, Customize** command, click the **Commands** tab and select **Macros** from the **Categories** list of the displayed dialogue box, shown in Fig. 12.6 below.

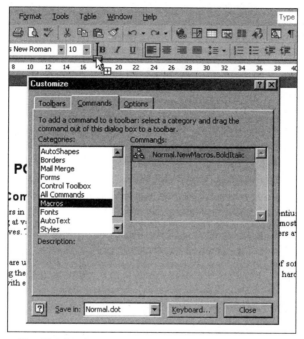

Fig. 12.6 Dragging a Macro Button onto a Word Toolbar

Next, click the macro from the **Commands** list and drag the button pointer onto one of the toolbars, as shown above. The macro inserts its *name* at the toolbar location pointed to by the vertical line on the toolbar as soon as you release the mouse button (before the **Bold** toolbar button above).

The macro name takes up much too much room on the toolbar, so click the **Modify Selection** button which has been added to the Customize dialogue box, select the **Change Button Image** option from the displayed menu list and choose a button from the palette shown on your screen (we chose the smiling face), as shown in Fig. 12.7 below.

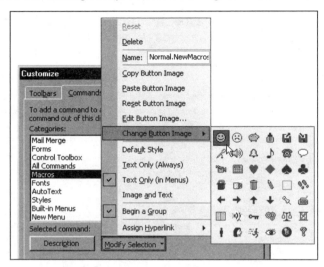

Fig. 12.7 Changing the Macro Button Image

Finally, you can select to display only the button on the toolbar by clicking the **Text Only (in Menus)**, as we have above, or to display both the button and its description by clicking the **Image and Text** option.

When you **Close** the Customize dialogue box you should have a new and fully functional toolbar button, like ours shown here. Even the screen tip works when you move the pointer over it!

In general, you can create toolbar buttons for commands and frequently used styles, AutoText entries, and fonts. For more detail on this subject, look up the 'Add or Remove Toolbar Buttons' section further on in this chapter.

## Removing Macro or Command Buttons

To remove a macro or command button from a toolbar, use the **Tools, Customize** commad, click the **Commands** tab and drag the button representing your macro or command from its position on the toolbar on to the editing area of your document.

## Editing a Macro

You can edit the entries in a macro file by selecting the **Tools**, **Macro**, **Macros**, command which opens the Macro dialogue box, shown in Fig. 12.4. Select the macro you want to edit and press the **Edit** button. This opens the Visual Basic for Applications Editor with the macro contents open for editing. The listing of our **Macro 1** file should look like that in Fig. 12.8 below:

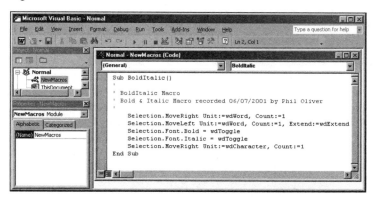

Fig. 12.8 The Visual Basic Editor

If you look at this listing you will see that it would be very easy to edit the commands in the file. If you do edit it, you should then save the file with the **File, Save Normal** command.

Macros within Visual Basic are considered to be 'subroutines' that run under an Office XP application, Word 2002 in this case.

It is easy to make small changes to macros you have recorded using the Visual Basic for Applications Editor.

However, if you wanted to create a macro that executed commands which could not be recorded, such as switching to a particular folder and displaying the Open dialogue box, then you must learn to use the Visual Basic programming language itself. That is something that is beyond the scope of this book. You could, try another of our books *Using Visual Basic* (BP498) which is also published by Bernard Babani (publishing) Ltd. It was not written with the Applications version of Visual Basic in mind, but the principles are the same.

To return to your document from a Visual Basic screen, click the Word icon at the top-left corner of the toolbar.

## Getting Help with Macros

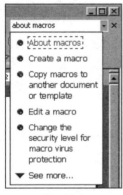

Fig. 12.9
About Macros

There is much more to macros than we could hope to cover in a general book on Word, so we suggest you type 'about macros' into the Ask a Question box of Word and press the <Enter> key. This opens a drop-down list of relevant help topics, as shown in Fig. 12.9 alongside. The more we use the Word help system, the more we realise that this is the easiest way to find useful topics. In fact Ask a Question help seems to locate topics that do not surface if you search in the Help system itself!

Do spend some time looking up each topic in turn. Once the main Help system is open there is also a lot of browsing to do there.

If you have installed the complete Word 2002 package, then you will have access to the full Visual Basic for Applications Help by using the **Help** menu option from the Visual Basic Editor. The opening window arrangement is shown next in Fig. 12.10

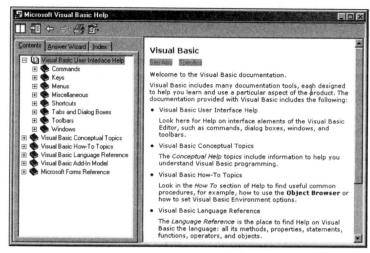

Fig. 12.10 The Visual Basic for Applications Help System

Within the help topics listed above, you should find a wealth of information, showing you how to program your macros and how to use the various built-in functions.

# Customising Toolbars and Menus

We have already touched on the subject of customising a Word toolbar when we showed you how to place a macro button on one. What follows is a more detailed account of how you can customise both toolbars and menus to your specific requirements, including the creation of your own toolbar.

Word 2002, as well as all the other components of Office XP, provide you with 'intelligent' toolbars and menus that monitor the way you work and make sure that the tools you use most often are available to you on them.

However, if you want to use some new tool which is not on a displayed toolbar or menu, you are in trouble - you will have to look for it amongst a wealth of tools which can be activated in a number of different ways! What we will try to do here, is to show you how you could increase your working efficiency, in the shortest possible time.

## The Default Toolbars and Menus

Fig. 12.11
Word Toolbars

A toolbar can contain buttons with images, menus, or a combination of both. Word includes many built-in toolbars that you can show and hide as needed by using the **View, Toolbars** command which opens the cascade menu shown to the left. To activate a toolbar, left-click it, which causes a small check mark to appear against it. By default, the Standard and Formatting built-in toolbars are docked side by side below the menu bar.

You can move toolbars by dragging the move handle on a docked toolbar, shown here to the right, or drag the title bar on a floating toolbar to another location. If you drag the toolbar to the edge of the program window or to a location beside another docked toolbar, it becomes a docked toolbar.

As we have seen in earlier chapters, when you first start Word, both active toolbars and short menus display standard buttons and basic commands. As you work with the program, the buttons and commands that you use most often are displayed on the toolbars and short menus. Both toolbars and menus can be expanded to show more buttons and commands by simply clicking the ⁑ **Toolbar Options** button at the end of the toolbar, or the ⹉ (double-arrow) at the bottom of the short menu.

To show the full set of buttons on a toolbar (if your working window is not long enough), drag the toolbar to a location other than the edge of the program window. To see more toolbars than those displayed when using the **View, Toolbars** command, use the **Tools, Customize** command to open the Customize dialogue box (Fig. 12.12), but click the **Toolbars** tab. We had a choice of 30 toolbars, even one to produce Japanese phrases!

To show the full set of menu commands, click the **Options** tab of the Customize dialogue box, shown below, then check and/or uncheck options as required.

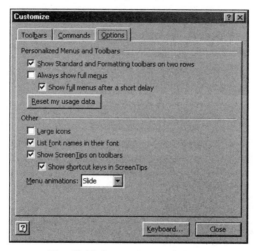

Fig. 12.12 Customisation Options

## Move or Copy Toolbar Buttons

If you wish to move or copy a toolbar button from one toolbar to another, use the **View, Toolbars** command and check both toolbars, so they are visible on your screen. Then do one of the following:

- To move a toolbar button, hold down the <Alt> key and drag the button to the new location on the same toolbar or onto another toolbar.

- To copy a toolbar button, hold down both the <Ctrl+Alt> keys and drag the button to the new location.

## Add or Remove Toolbar Buttons

To add a button to a toolbar, first display the toolbar in question, then use the **Tools**, **Customize** command to open the Customize dialogue box, shown in Fig. 12.13 below, with the **Commands** tab selected.

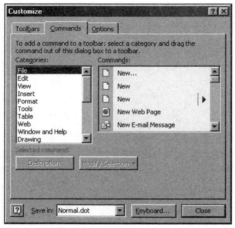

Fig. 12.13 Adding Commands to a Word Toolbar

Then do the following:

- In the **Categories** box, click a category for the command you want the button to perform. For example, click Macros to add a button that runs a macro, click Styles to add a button that applies a style, click AutoText to add a button that inserts an AutoText entry, or click Fonts to add a button that applies a particular font.

- Drag the command or macro you want from the **Commands** box to the displayed toolbar.

If you don't see the command you want under a particular category, click All Commands in the **Categories** box.

To quickly add a built-in button to a built-in toolbar, click on ▪ (**Toolbar Options**), then click **Add or Remove Buttons**, choose the toolbar name, and select the check box next to the button you want to add.

To remove a button from a displayed toolbar, hold the <Alt> button down and drag the unwanted button from its position on the toolbar on to the editing area of your document. When you remove a built-in toolbar button, the button is still available in the Customize dialogue box. However, when you remove a custom toolbar button, it is permanently deleted. To remove and save a custom toolbar button for later use, you should create a 'storage toolbar' as described below.

## Create a Custom Toolbar

To create a custom toolbar, carry out the following steps:

*   Display the toolbars that contain the buttons (whether custom or built-in buttons) you want to copy, move, or store in a custom toolbar.

*   Use the **Tools**, **Customize** command, and click the **Toolbars** tab of the displayed dialogue box.

*   Click the **New** button to display the screen shown below.

Fig. 12.14 Creating a New Customised Toolbar

- In the **Toolbar name** text box, type the name you want, and in the **Make toolbar available to** box, click the template or document you want to save the toolbar in, and then click **OK**.

- Finally, click the **Close** button. The new toolbar remains showing on the screen.

You can now use the skills acquired earlier to move and/or copy buttons to the new toolbar. If the newly created toolbar is for 'storing' deleted custom-made buttons, then you will probably want to hide it by right-clicking it and clearing the check box next to its name in the shortcut menu.

## Manipulating Menu Commands

Menu commands can be added to or removed from menus in the same way as buttons can be added to or removed from toolbars. You could even add menus to a button on a toolbar.

For example, to add a command or other item to a menu, do the following:

- Use the **Tools**, **Customize** command to open the Customize dialogue box, and click the **Commands** tab.

- In the **Categories** box, click a category for the command.

- Drag the command you want from the **Commands** box over the menu. When the menu displays a list of menu options, point to the location where you want the command to appear on the menu, and then release the mouse, as shown in Fig. 12.15 on the next page.

If you don't see the command you want under a particular category, click All Commands in the Categories box.

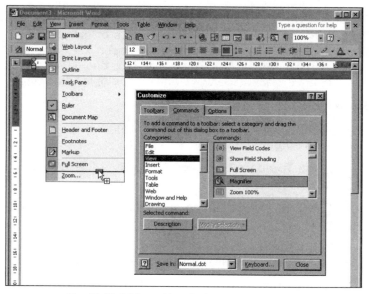

Fig. 12.15 Adding a New Option to a Word Menu

To remove a command from a list of menu options, do the following:

- Open the Customize dialogue box (you might have to move it out of the way of the drop-down menu options from which you want to remove a command).

- Select the menu option you want to remove and drag it to the editing area of your document.

- Release the mouse button to delete the unwanted menu option.

As you can see, manipulating menu options is very similar to manipulating buttons on toolbars, so we leave it to you to explore all the available possibilities - have fun!

## Restoring Default Toolbars or Menus

To restore the default buttons on toolbars or menu options, use the **Tools**, **Customize** command to open the Customize dialogue box. Leave the Customize box open (you might need to move it out of the way), and do one of the following:

***For a toolbar:***

- Use the **Tools, Customize** command, and then click the **Toolbars** tab.

- In the **Toolbars** box, click the name of the toolbar you want to reset original buttons and menus on.

- Click the **Reset** button to open the Reset Toolbar dialogue box.

- In the **Reset changes...** text box, click the template or document that contains the changes you want to reset.

***For a menu:***

- Use the **Tools, Customize** command, and then click the Commands tab.

- Click the menu that contains the command you want to restore. Right-click the menu command, and then click **Reset** on the shortcut menu.

## Getting Help on Toolbars and Menus

Fig. 12.16
About Menus

Word 2002 has several help screens on toolbars and menus. To look at some of these, simply search for 'menus' in the Ask a Question box. This returns the list of topics shown here.

We suggest you spend some time looking at the various help topics. For example, clicking the third entry under 'About menus', opens the Microsoft Word Help screen shown in Fig. 12.17 on the next page.

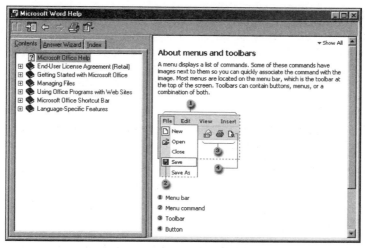

Fig. 12.17 Help on Menus and Toolbars

********************

That is about it. We hope you have enjoyed reading this book as much as we have enjoyed writing it. Of course Word 2002 is capable of a lot more than we have discussed here, but what we have tried to do is to give you enough information so that you can forge ahead and explore by yourself the rest of its capabilities.

A glossary is included next, for reference, and in case you have trouble with any jargon that may have crept in.

# 13

# Glossary of Terms

ActiveX

A set of technologies that enables software components to interact with one another in a networked environment, regardless of the language in which the components were created.

Add-in

A mini-program which runs in conjunction with another and enhances its functionality.

Address

A unique number or name that identifies a specific computer or user on a network.

Anonymous FTP

Anonymous FTP allows you to connect to a remote computer and transfer public files back to your local computer without the need to have a user ID and password.

ANSI

American National Standards Institute. A US government organisation responsible for improving communication standards.

Application

Software (program) designed to carry out certain activity, such as word processing, or data management.

Applet

A program that can be downloaded over a network and launched on the user's computer.

| | |
|---|---|
| Archie | Archie is an Internet service that allows you to locate files that can be downloaded via FTP. |
| ASP | Active Server Page. File format used for dynamic Web pages that get their data from a server based database. |
| Association | An identification of a filename extension to a program. This lets Windows open the program when its files are selected. |
| ASCII | A binary code representation of a character set. The name stands for 'American Standard Code for Information Interchange'. |
| Attachment | A file that is added to an e-mail message for transmission. |
| Authoring | The process of creating web documents or software. |
| AVI | Audio Video Interleaved. A Windows multimedia file format for sound and moving pictures. |
| Backbone | The main transmission lines of the Internet, running at over 45Mbps (million bits per second). |
| Background | An image, colour or texture which forms the background of a Web page or document. |
| Backup | To make a back-up copy of a file or a disc for safekeeping. |
| Bandwidth | The range of transmission frequencies a network can use. The greater the bandwidth the more information that can be transferred over a network. |

| | |
|---|---|
| Banner | An advertising graphic shown on a Web page. |
| BASIC | Beginner's All-purpose Symbolic Instruction Code - a high-level programming language. |
| BBS | Bulletin Board System, a computer equipped with software and telecoms links that allow it to act as an information host for remote computer systems. |
| Beta test | A test of software that is still under development, by people actually using the software. |
| BinHex | A file conversion format that converts binary files to ASCII text files. |
| Bitmap | A technique for managing the image displayed on a computer screen. |
| Bookmark | A marker inserted at a specific point in a document. Used as a target for a hypertext link, or to enable a user to return for later reference. |
| Bound control | A control on a database form, report or data access page that is tied to a field in an underlying table or query. |
| Browse | A button in some Windows dialogue boxes that lets you view a list of files and folders before you make a selection. Also to view a Web page. |
| Browser | A program, like the Internet Explorer, that lets you view Web pages. |
| Bug | An error in coding or logic that causes a program to malfunction. |

| | |
|---|---|
| Button | A graphic element or icon in a dialogue box or toolbar that performs a specified function. |
| Cache | An area of memory, or disc space, reserved for data, which speeds up downloading. |
| Card | A removable printed-circuit board that is plugged into a computer expansion slot. |
| CD-ROM | Compact Disc - Read Only Memory; an optical disc which information may be read from but not written to. |
| CGI | Common Gateway Interface - a convention for servers to communicate with local applications and allow users to provide information to scripts attached to web pages, usually through forms. |
| Cgi-bin | The most common name of a directory on a web server in which CGI programs are stored. |
| Chart | A graphical view of data that is used to visually display trends, patterns, and comparisons. |
| Click | To press and release a mouse button once without moving the mouse. |
| Client | A computer that has access to services over a computer network. The computer providing the services is a server. |
| Client application | A Windows application that can accept linked, or embedded, objects. |
| Clipboard | A temporary storage area of memory, where text and graphics are stored with the cut and copy actions. The |

|  | Office XP clipboard can store up to 24 items. |
|---|---|
| Command | An instruction given to a computer to carry out a particular action. |
| Compressed file | One that is compacted to save server space and reduce transfer times. Typical file extensions for compressed files include .zip (DOS/Windows) and .tar (UNIX). |
| Configuration | A general purpose term referring to the way you have your computer set up. |
| Context menu | A menu that opens when you right-click the mouse button on a feature. |
| Controls | Objects on a form, report, or data access page that display data, perform actions, or are used for decoration. |
| Cookies | Files stored on your hard drive by your Web browser that hold information for it to use. |
| CPU | The Central Processing Unit; the main chip that executes all instructions entered into a computer. |
| Cyberspace | Originated by William Gibson in his novel 'Neuromancer', now used to describe the Internet and the other computer networks. |
| Data access page | A Web page, created by Access, that has a connection to a database; you can view, add, edit, and manipulate the data in this page. |
| Database | A collection of data related to a particular topic or purpose. |

DBMS

Database management system - A software interface between the database and the user.

Dial-up Connection

A popular form of Net connection for the home user, over standard telephone lines.

Direct Connection

A permanent connection between your computer system and the Internet.

Default

The command, device or option automatically chosen.

Desktop

The Windows screen working background, on which you place icons, folders, etc.

Device driver

A special file that must be loaded into memory for Windows to be able to address a specific procedure or hardware device.

Device name

A logical name used by an operating system to identify a device, such as LPT1 or COM1 for the parallel or serial printer.

Dialogue box

A window displayed on the screen to allow the user to enter information.

Directory

An area on disc where information relating to a group of files is kept. Also known as a folder.

Disc

A device on which you can store programs and data.

Disconnect

To detach a drive, port or computer from a shared device, or to break an Internet connection.

Document

A file produced by an application program. When used in reference to the Web, a document is any file containing text, media or hyperlinks that can be transferred from an HTTP server to a browser.

Domain
A group of devices, servers and computers on a network.

Domain Name
The name of an Internet site, for example www.michaelstrang.com, which allows you to reference Internet sites without knowing their true numerical address.

DOS
Disc Operating System. A collection of small specialised programs that allow interaction between user and computer.

Double-click
To quickly press and release a mouse button twice.

Download
To transfer to your computer a file, or data, from another computer.

DPI
Dots Per Inch - a resolution standard for laser printers.

Drag
To move an object on the screen by pressing and holding down the left mouse button while moving the mouse.

Drive name
The letter followed by a colon which identifies a floppy or hard disc drive.

Drop-down list
A menu item that can be clicked to open extra items that can be selected.

EISA
Extended Industry Standard Architecture, for construction of PCs with the Intel 32-bit micro-processor.

Embedded object
Information in a document that is 'copied' from its source application. Selecting the object opens the

|               | creating application from within the document. |
|---------------|-----------------|
| Engine        | Software used by search services. |
| E-mail        | Electronic Mail - A system that allows computer users to send and receive messages electronically. |
| Ethernet      | A very common method of networking computers in a LAN. |
| FAQ           | Frequently Asked Questions - A common feature on the Internet, FAQs are files of answers to commonly asked questions. |
| FAT           | The File Allocation Table. An area on disc where information is kept on which part of the disc a file is located. |
| File extension | The suffix following the period in a filename. Windows uses this to identify the source application program. For example **.mdb** indicates a Microsoft Access file. |
| Filename      | The name given to a file. In Windows 95 and above this can be up to 256 characters long. |
| Filter        | A set of criteria that is applied to data to show a subset of the data. |
| Firewall      | Security measures designed to protect a networked system from unauthorised access. |
| Floppy disc   | A removable disc on which information can be stored magnetically. |
| Folder        | An area used to store a group of files, usually with a common link. |

| | |
|---|---|
| Font | A graphic design representing a set of characters, numbers and symbols. |
| Freeware | Software that is available for downloading and unlimited use without charge. |
| FTP | File Transfer Protocol. The procedure for connecting to a remote computer and transferring files. |
| Function key | One of the series of 10 or 12 keys marked with the letter F and a numeral, used for specific operations. |
| Gateway | A computer system that allows otherwise incompatible networks to communicate with each other. |
| GIF | Graphics Interchange Format, a common standard for images on the Web. |
| Graphic | A picture or illustration, also called an image. Formats include GIF, JPEG, BMP, PCX, and TIFF. |
| Graphics card | A device that controls the display on the monitor and other allied functions. |
| GUI | A Graphic User Interface, such as Windows 98, the software front-end meant to provide an attractive and easy to use interface. |
| Hard copy | Output on paper. |
| Hard disc | A device built into the computer for holding programs and data. |
| Hardware | The equipment that makes up a computer system, excluding the programs or software. |

| | |
|---|---|
| Help | A Windows system that gives you instructions and additional information on using a program. |
| Helper application | A program allowing you to view multimedia files that your web browser cannot handle internally. |
| Hit | A single request from a web browser for a single item from a web server. |
| Home page | The document displayed when you first open your Web browser, or the first document you come to at a Web site. |
| Host | Computer connected directly to the Internet that provides services to other local and/or remote computers. |
| Hotlist | A list of frequently used Web locations and URL addresses. |
| Host | A computer acting as an information or communications server. |
| HTML | HyperText Markup Language, the format used in documents on the Web. |
| HTML editor | Authoring tool which assists with the creation of HTML pages. |
| HTTP | HyperText Transport Protocol, the system used to link and transfer hypertext documents on the Web. |
| Hyperlink | A segment of text, or an image, that refers to another document on the Web, an Intranet or your PC. |
| Hypermedia | Hypertext extended to include linked multimedia. |
| Hypertext | A system that allows documents to be cross-linked so that the reader can |

explore related links, or documents, by clicking on a highlighted symbol.

Icon

A small graphic image, or button, that represents a function or object. Clicking on an icon produces an action.

Image

See graphic.

Insertion point

A flashing bar that shows where typed text will be entered into a document.

Interface

A device that allows you to connect a computer to its peripherals.

Internet

The global system of computer networks.

Intranet

A private network inside an organisation using the same kind of software as the Internet.

ISA

Industry Standard Architecture; a standard for internal connections in PCs.

ISDN

Integrated Services Digital Network, a telecom standard using digital transmission technology to support voice, video and data communications applications over regular telephone lines.

IP

Internet Protocol - The rules that provide basic Internet functions.

IP Address

Internet Protocol Address - every computer on the Internet has a unique identifying number.

ISDN

Integrated Services Digital Network. A fast communications network operating at a minimum of 64 Kbps (thousand bits per second).

| | |
|---|---|
| ISP | Internet Service Provider - A company that offers access to the Internet. |
| Java | An object-oriented programming language created by Sun Microsystems for developing applications and applets that are capable of running on any computer, regardless of the operating system. |
| JPEG/JPG | Joint Photographic Experts Group, a popular cross-platform format for image files. JPEG is best suited for true colour original images. |
| Kilobyte | (KB); 1024 bytes of information or storage space. |
| LAN | Local Area Network - High-speed, privately-owned network covering a limited geographical area, such as an office or a building. |
| Laptop | A portable computer small enough to sit on your lap. |
| LCD | Liquid Crystal Display. |
| Links | The hypertext connections between Web pages. |
| Local | A resource that is located on your computer, not linked to it over a network. |
| Location | An Internet address. |
| Log on | To gain access to a network. |
| MCI | Media Control Interface - a standard for files and multimedia devices. |
| Megabyte | (MB); 1024 kilobytes of information or storage space. |

| | |
|---|---|
| Megahertz | (MHz); Speed of processor in millions of cycles per second. |
| Memory | Part of computer consisting of storage elements organised into addressable locations that can hold data and instructions. |
| Menu | A list of available options in an application. |
| Menu bar | The horizontal bar that lists the names of menus. |
| MIDI | Musical Instrument Digital Interface - enables devices to transmit and receive sound and music messages. |
| MIME | Multipurpose Internet Mail Extensions, a messaging standard that allows Internet users to exchange e-mail messages enhanced with graphics, video and voice. |
| MIPS | Million Instructions Per Second; measures speed of a system. |
| Modem | Short for Modulator-demodulator devices. An electronic device that lets computers communicate electronically. |
| Monitor | The display device connected to your PC, also called a screen. |
| Mouse | A device used to manipulate a pointer around your display and activate processes by pressing buttons. |
| MPEG | Motion Picture Experts Group - a video file format offering excellent quality in a relatively small file. |
| MS-DOS | Microsoft's implementation of the Disc Operating System for PCs. |

| | |
|---|---|
| Multimedia | The use of photographs, music and sound and movie images in a presentation. |
| Multi-tasking | Performing more than one operation at the same time. |
| Network | Two or more computers connected together to share resources. |
| Network server | Central computer which stores files for several linked computers. |
| Node | Any single computer connected to a network. |
| ODBC | Open DataBase Connectivity - A standard protocol for accessing information in a SQL database server. |
| OLE | Object Linking and Embedding - A technology for transferring and sharing information among software applications. |
| Online | Having access to the Internet. |
| On-line Service | Services such as America On-line and CompuServe that provide content to subscribers and usually connections to the Internet. |
| Operating system | Software that runs a computer. |
| Page | An HTML document, or Web site. |
| Password | A unique character string used to gain access to a network, program, or mailbox. |
| PATH | The location of a file in the directory tree. |
| Peripheral | Any device attached to a PC. |

| | |
|---|---|
| Perl | A popular language for programming CGI applications. |
| PIF file | Program information file - gives information to Windows about an MS-DOS application. |
| Pixel | A picture element on screen; the smallest element that can be independently assigned colour and intensity. |
| Plug-and-play | Hardware which can be plugged into a PC and be used immediately without configuration. |
| POP3 | Post Office Protocol - a method of storing and returning e-mail. |
| Port | The place where information goes into or out of a computer, e.g. a modem might be connected to the serial port. |
| PPP | Point-to-Point Protocol - One of two methods (see SLIP) for using special software to establish a temporary direct connection to the Internet over regular phone lines. |
| Print queue | A list of print jobs waiting to be sent to a printer. |
| Program | A set of instructions which cause a computer to perform tasks. |
| Protocol | A set of rules or standards that define how computers communicate with each other. |
| Query | The set of keywords and operators sent by a user to a search engine, or a database search request. |

| Queue | A list of e-mail messages waiting to be sent over the Internet. |
| --- | --- |
| RAM | Random Access Memory. The computer's volatile memory. Data held in it is lost when power is switched off. |
| Real mode | MS-DOS mode, typically used to run programs, such as MS-DOS games, that will not run under Windows. |
| Resource | A directory, or printer, that can be shared over a network. |
| Right-click | To click the right mouse button once. |
| Robot | A Web agent that visits sites, by requesting documents from them, for the purposes of indexing for search engines. Also known as Wanderers, Crawlers, or Spiders. |
| ROM | Read Only Memory. A PC's non-volatile memory. Data is written into this memory at manufacture and is not affected by power loss. |
| RTF | Rich Text Format. An enhanced form of text that includes basic formatting and is used for transferring data between applications, or in e-mail messages. |
| Scroll bar | A bar that appears at the right side or bottom edge of a window. |
| Search | Submit a query to a search engine. |
| Search engine | A program that helps users find information across the Internet. |
| Serial interface | An interface that transfers data as individual bits. |

| | |
|---|---|
| Server | A computer system that manages and delivers information for client computers. |
| Shared resource | Any device, program or file that is available to network users. |
| Shareware | Software that is available on public networks and bulletin boards. Users are expected to pay a nominal amount to the software developer. |
| Signature file | An ASCII text file, maintained within e-mail programs, that contains text for your signature. |
| Site | A place on the Internet. Every Web page has a location where it resides which is called its site. |
| SLIP | Serial Line Internet Protocol, a method of Internet connection that enables computers to use phone lines and a modem to connect to the Internet without having to connect to a host. |
| Smart tag | New to Office XP. A button that when clicked, opens a shortcut menu to give fast access to other features or Office applications. |
| SMTP | Simple Mail Transfer Protocol - a protocol dictating how e-mail messages are exchanged over the Internet. |
| Socket | An endpoint for sending and receiving data between computers. |
| Software | The programs and instructions that control your PC. |
| Spamming | Sending the same message to a large number of mailing lists or |

|  |  |
|---|---|
|  | newsgroups. Also to overload a Web page with excessive keywords in an attempt to get a better search ranking. |
| Spider | See robot. |
| Spooler | Software which handles transfer of information to a store to be used by a peripheral device. |
| SQL | Structured Query Language, used with relational databases. |
| SSL | Secure Sockets Layer, the standard transmission security protocol developed by Netscape, which has been put into the public domain. |
| Subscribe | To become a member of. |
| Surfing | The process of looking around the Internet. |
| SVGA | Super Video Graphics Array; it has all the VGA modes but with 256, or more, colours. |
| Swap file | An area of your hard disc used to store temporary operating files, also known as virtual memory. |
| Sysop | System Operator - A person responsible for the physical operations of a computer system or network resource. |
| System disc | A disc containing files to enable a PC to start up. |
| T1 | An Internet leased line that carries up to 1.536 million bits per second (1.536 Mbps). |

| | |
|---|---|
| T3 | An Internet leased line that carries up to 45 million bits per second (45 Mbps). |
| Task bar | The bar that by default is located at the bottom of your screen whenever Windows is running. It contains the Start button, buttons for all the applications that are open, and icons for other applications. |
| Task Pane | A pane or sub-window that gives a range of options pertaining to the task currently being performed. New to Office XP applications. |
| TCP/IP | Transmission Control Protocol/ Internet Protocol, combined protocols that perform the transfer of data between two computers. TCP monitors and ensures the correct transfer of data. IP receives the data, breaks it up into packets, and sends it to a network within the Internet. |
| Telnet | A program which allows people to remotely use computers across networks. |
| Text file | An unformatted file of text characters saved in ASCII format. |
| Thread | An ongoing message-based conversation on a single subject. |
| Thumbnail | A small graphic image. |
| TIFF | Tag Image File Format - a popular graphic image file format. |
| Tool | Software program used to support Web site creation and management. |
| Toolbar | A bar containing buttons or icons giving quick access to commands. |

| Toggle | To turn an action on and off with the same switch. |
| TrueType fonts | Fonts that can be scaled to any size and print as they show on the screen. |
| UNC | Universal Naming Convention - A convention for files that provides a machine independent means of locating the file that is particularly useful in Web based applications. |
| UNIX | Multitasking, multi-user computer operating system that is run by many computers that are connected to the Internet. Linux is a version of Unix. |
| Upload/Download | The process of transferring files between computers. Files are uploaded from your computer to another and downloaded from another computer to your own. |
| URL | Uniform Resource Locator, the addressing system used on the Web, containing information about the method of access, the server to be accessed and the path of the file to be accessed. |
| Usenet | Informal network of computers that allow the posting and reading of messages in newsgroups that focus on specific topics. |
| User ID | The unique identifier, usually used in conjunction with a password, which identifies you on a computer. |
| Virtual Reality | Simulations of real or imaginary worlds, rendered on a flat two-dimensional screen but appearing three-dimensional. |

| | |
|---|---|
| Virus | A malicious program, downloaded from a web site or disc, designed to wipe out information on your computer. |
| Watermark | Toned down image or text that appears in the background of a printed page. |
| W3C | The World Wide Web Consortium that is steering standards development for the Web. |
| WAIS | Wide Area Information Server, a Net-wide system for looking up specific information in Internet databases. |
| WAV | Waveform Audio (**.wav**) - a common audio file format for DOS/Windows computers. |
| Web | A network of hypertext-based multimedia information servers. Browsers are used to view any information on the Web. |
| Web Page | An HTML document that is accessible on the Web. |
| Webmaster | One whose job it is to manage a web site. |
| WINSOCK | A Microsoft Windows file that provides the interface to TCP/IP services. |
| Wizard | A Microsoft tool that shows how to perform certain operations, or asks you questions and then creates an object depending on your answers. |

# Index

**Notes**

# Companion Discs

COMPANION DISCS are available for many of the computer books written by the same author(s) and published by BERNARD BABANI (publishing) LTD, as listed at the front of this book (except for those marked with an asterisk). These books contain many pages of file/program listings. There is no reason why you should spend hours typing them into your computer, unless you wish to do so, or need the practice.

## ORDERING INSTRUCTIONS

To obtain companion discs, fill in the order form below, or a copy of it, enclose a cheque (payable to **P.R.M. Oliver**) or a postal order, and send it to the address given below. **Make sure you fill in your name and address** and specify the book number and title in your order.

| Book No. | Book Name | Unit Price | Total Price |
|---|---|---|---|
| BP ........ | | £3.50 | |
| BP ........ | | £3.50 | |
| BP ........ | | £3.50 | |
| Name ............................. | | Sub-total | £............ |
| Address ............................. | | P & P (@ 45p/disc) | £............ |
| | | | |
| | | Total Due | £............ |

**Send to: P.R.M. Oliver, West Trevarth House, West Trevarth Nr Redruth, Cornwall TR16 5TJ**

**PLEASE NOTE**

The author(s) are fully responsible for providing this Companion Disc service. The publishers of this book accept no responsibility for the supply, quality, or magnetic contents of the disc, or in respect of any damage, or injury that might be suffered or caused by its use.